PREACHING UPSTREAM

Reflections on Preaching and the
Word of God in Current Times

DR. JERRY M. CARTER

Dear Lee,

So thankful for you and your service and brotherhood for several years!

Blessings –

P. Ga

Preaching Upstream: Reflections on Preaching and the Word of God in Current Times
By Dr. Jerry M. Carter

Copyright © Jerry M. Carter

Published 2024

No part of this book shall be reproduced, stored in a retrieval system, or transmitted by any means, electronic, mechanical, photocopying, recording, or otherwise, without written permission from the publisher, except for brief quotations in printed reviews. No patent liability is assumed with respect to the use of the information contained herein. Although every precaution has been taken in the preparation of this book, the publisher and author assume no responsibility for errors or omissions. Neither is any liability assumed for damages resulting from the use of the information contained herein.

For information, address:
The Church Online, LLC
1000 Ardmore Blvd.
Pittsburgh, PA 15221

International Standard Book Number:
978-1-68548-016-5

Library of Congress Catalogue Card Number:
Available Upon Request

Printed in the United States of America

-Unless otherwise indicated, Scripture quotations are taken from the Holy Bible, New King James Version®. Copyright © 1982 by Thomas Nelson, Inc. Used by permission. All rights reserved.

Scripture quotations marked NRSV taken from the New Revised Standard Version, Updated Edition. Copyright © 2021 National Council of Churches of Christ in the United States of America. Used by permission. All rights reserved worldwide.

Scripture quotations marked KJV taken from the New King James Version of the Bible. Public Domain.

Table of Contents

09   *Chapter One:*
Preaching Upstream

27   *Chapter Two:*
No More Home Field Advantage

43   *Chapter Three:*
Reimagining Expository Preaching

63   *Chapter Four:*
Magnetic Preaching

81   *Chapter Five:*
Under the Broom Tree: Managing the Post-Partum Blues

97 *Chapter Six:*
A Refusal to Go to Hell in Peace: The Role of the Prophet/Preacher in Raising the Moral Conscience of the Nation

117 *Chapter Seven:*
Keep Your Turban On: The Challenge and Necessity of Preaching through Adversity

135 *Chapter Eight:*
Beyond Mechanics: Accessing Power for Preaching

151 *Chapter Nine:*
From Fans to Followers: A Textual Consideration of the Aim of Pulpit Preaching

173 *Chapter Ten:*
Are We Bored with Jesus?

195 *Chapter Eleven:*
Unrolling the Scroll: Reclaiming Evangelical Preaching:

213   *Chapter Twelve:*
A Pregnant Silence: Disconnecting in Order to Connect

227   *Chapter Thirteen:*
Over Flow Preaching: "Go Get it, Eat it, and Preach it"

243   *Chapter Fourteen:*
Standing in the Assembly: A Reconsideration of the Place and Future of Preaching

269   **Biography**

271   **Bibliography**

Chapter One

Preaching Upstream
2 TIM. 4:2 NKJV

One of the most amazing phenomena of nature is the journey of salmon and some other kinds of fish swimming upstream. The salmon spends most of its life in a saltwater environment. But when it's time to spawn, salmon return with uncanny precision to the natal river where they were born. They follow a familiar scent that leads them back to the location of their birth. In order to do this, they literally have to swim against the current. Something within them leads them back to where they were born. Some salmon even swim up waterfalls. It's impossible for them to do what they are intended to do unless they are willing to swim against the current of nature. It's impossible for them to "swim" into purpose without being willing to swim upstream.

"Swimming upstream" has become an idiomatic expression meaning to opt for a difficult course of action when a simpler, safer alternative is available. It is no stretch to say that preaching is akin to swimming upstream. Out of necessity, every time we stand to declare the "euangelion" we are preaching upstream. Preaching that flows too easily downstream is probably not the gospel of Jesus Christ. To some extent, preaching is always an upstream engagement because real preaching is always counter cultural. Walter Brueggemann was correct when he said that on Sunday mornings the preacher offers an alternative world that is radically different from the world in which people live. Elijah, the unrefined prophet from Tishbe, preached upstream when he challenged King Ahab. Jeremiah, the prophet of passion, was warned by Jehovah from the outset that he would be preaching upstream, "See, I have this day set you over the nations and

Chapter One

over the kingdoms, to root out, and to pull down, and to destroy, and to throw down, to build and to plant" (Jer. 1:10, NKJV). Amos of Tekoa preached upstream when he declared in Amos 5:24, "But let justice run down as waters, and righteousness as a mighty stream" (NKJV). Mary Magdalene journeyed and preached upstream when she took news of the resurrection to unbelieving disciples. Paul knew he was preaching upstream when he said in 1 Cor. 18 "For the preaching of the cross is... foolishness..." (KJV). Jesus ended up on a cross in part because he preached "upstream." Martin Luther in the Reformation, Bonhoeffer in Germany, Mary Lena Lewis Tate a Black woman protest preacher in Tennessee in the early 1900's, Richard Allen in Philadelphia, Martin King in Montgomery, Desmond Tutu in South Africa, along with a host of others too numerous to name were all upstream preachers. Inherently and of necessity, preaching must swim upstream.

Preaching in today's context is especially "upstream", because of the landscape surrounding the church and the landscape within the church. These are strange times. We preach in a time of Christless ecumenism, religion-less spiritualism, and sanctified consumerism. There is an excessive focus on seeker sensitivity, empty diversity, political correctness, and cultural atheism. Tithing is down within our churches. Attendance is not what it used to be. Within the last seven years, those who describe themselves as Christians in this country have dropped by nearly 8%. Contrastingly, Atheists, Agnostics, and the unaffiliated have risen 6% in the same time period. Church-going folks are getting older and the unaffiliated are getting younger. In some cases, more people are watching church on computer screens and smart devices than are actually in the seats. Younger believers do not feel a need to come to a church nor be involved in institutional religion. "Spirituality" is posited as a deeper faith reality than is the idea of religion. Whatever brand of spirituality you want is as available as coffee flavors. Leonard Sweet once said that there are those in and around our churches who do not realize that spirituality without embodied expression in a religious community is not much more than inverted narcissism. Our preaching must "swim" upstream, against the current of the culture.

Chapter One

As disheartening as some of this sounds, we should not be surprised because Paul warns Timothy in 2 Timothy 4:3-4:

> For the time will come when they will not endure sound doctrine, but according to their own desires, because they have itching ears, they will heap up for themselves teachers; and they will turn their ears away from the truth, and be turned aside to fables. (NKJV)

Paul says the time will come. It is probably the case today that "will come" is now "has come." The time has come that, "...they do not endure sound doctrine..." The time has come that they gather around a multitude of teachers who offer a smorgasbord of faith options. The time has come that there is a turning away from truth and a turning toward fables. What Paul says "will come" has now actually come.

These are strange times, but ironically these are ideal times for the gospel of Jesus Christ. I was having lunch with the late Dr. Gardner Taylor several years ago and he said to me, "Preacher, I see strange days ahead, but these will be great days in which to preach." In this "upstream" journey, in this present context, this is what Paul says: "I charge you therefore before God and Lord Jesus Christ, who will judge the living and the dead at His appearing and His kingdom: Preach the Word! Be ready in season and out of season..." (2 Timothy 4:1-2). This is the calling of the preacher in this present landscape that has gone through a seismic shift. The charge is piercingly simple: "Preach the Word! Be ready in season and out of season..." No need for deep interpretation, it is painfully, almost insultingly simple.

Paul is very clear about **what we are to do** in this current climate. We must, "Preach the Word!" But there must be something more than this. This simplicity insults our intelligence and assaults our incessant search for new ways to preach. The Greek word for preach is Kerusso. It is the idea of heralding good news. The herald runs into town and urgently declares good news to the citizens. The herald is loud and intrusive. He or she cannot wait until the morning. The nature of news mandates an energetic, interruptive declaration. We have news from another network. We have "breaking news" that interrupts the normal flow of the week whenever the news is declared.

Chapter One

What are we to preach? "The Word!" We are to declare the core kerygma. We preach Jesus. Jesus is the center and circumference of what we preach. One preacher has rightly said that we live in a church age that suffers from JDD-Jesus Deficit Disorder. We cannot be afraid to name the Name. I understand that it might appear to be narrow in this pluralistic age; I understand that it might not be politically correct to say, but I yet believe what Luke says in Acts 4, "Neither is there salvation in any other: for there is none other name under heaven given among people, whereby we must be saved" (KJV). And when Peter was caught up in a moment of cultural pluralism on the top of the Mountain of Transfiguration, he wanted to build three tabernacles, one each, for Moses, Elijah, and Jesus as though they were all peers. The voice of God interrupted the moment and particularized and pinpointed His designated one and said, "This is my beloved Son, in whom I am well pleased. Hear ye Him" (Mat. 17:4-5, NKJV). The majestic, mesmerizing voice of God knocked Peter, James, and John to their knees. When they had enough strength to rise up, the only one left was Jesus.

Whatever we preach, it should lead to Jesus. In Jared C. Wilson's, *The 5 C's of Preaching*, Charles Spurgeon is quoted as saying to a young preacher:

> Don't you know, young man, that from every town and village and every hamlet in England, wherever it may be, there is a road to London?... and so from every text in Scripture there is a road to the metropolis of the Scriptures, this is, Christ. And my dear brother, your business is when you get to a text, to say, 'now, what is the road to Christ?' and then preach a sermon, running along the road towards the great metropolis-Christ...

Spurgeon goes on to say:

> I have never yet found a text that had not got a road to Christ in it, and if ever I do find one.... I will go over hedge and ditch but I would get at my Master, for the sermon cannot do any good unless there is a savor of Christ in it. (www.the gospelcoalition.org)

The road of Genesis leads to Christ. The route of Isaiah leads to Christ. The avenue of Ephesians leads to Christ. It may mean some upstream preaching, but whatever you do, get there. Preach the Word!

Paul is clear about **how we are to do what we do**. Preach the Word! Be ready in season and out of season. Preach the word with a constant readiness. The King James says, "Be instant." Other versions say, "Be ready." The Greek word is "Ephistemi". It literally means stand upon or stand up. Stand up and stand upon work together. The only way to stand up in some seasons is to stand upon. The word I am standing up with is the word I have to stand upon. You cannot stand up in certain seasons if you do not stand on the same word you are standing up with. If the word I am standing up with is Isaiah 26:3, "Thou will keep in perfect peace, those who's minds are stayed on you", then I need to stand upon that same word. To "be ready" means to "stand up" and "stand upon." The only way to preach upstream is to stand upon what you are standing up with.

Paul borrows this word from the world of the military. It carries the idea of "staying at your post." Your post is your pulpit. Your post is your preaching platform, whether it is before thousands in a megachurch environment or before five people at the nursing home or local prison. The command, in this upstream climate is to stay at your post. People may be joining, or they may not be joining but stay at your post. The money may be coming in or it may not be coming in but stay at your post. Endure hardness as a good soldier and stay at your post. The clouds of frustration and hopelessness may cloud your mental sky, but still stay at your post.

Stay at your post in season and out of season. Stand up and stand upon in season and out of season. The Word with which and on which we stand, covers us in all-weather conditions. Our gospel is not a "hot house" gospel. Hot house vegetables can only prosper and grow in the comfortable confines of a greenhouse. They can't prosper in changing weather. Our gospel is all weather and refers to external circumstances and internal disposition.

External circumstances are the changing seasons around us. "In season and out of season" are phrases/words which are almost exactly alike except for the prefix. "In season" is the word "eukairos". "Out of season" is the word "akairos." In both cases the root word is

Chapter One

"Kairos". "Kairos" is opportune moment. "Kairos" as opposed to "chronos", refers to season and not just time on the clock. "In season" literally means "pleasant times." "Out of season" is just the opposite, it means "unpleasant times." The gospel is built for "eukairos" moments and "akairos" moments.

Paul tells Timothy to "stand your post" in season and out of season. This was fitting for young Timothy because he was presently enduring a difficult season. Paul wrote this second letter when Timothy was experiencing adversity. A few years earlier, the picture had been radically different. At that time, the church of Ephesus was growing and thriving. Timothy was the new, young pastor whom the church loved. Those early years for Timothy were fun and eventful, and everything was moving. His members were inviting him over for dinner each Sunday. The church at Ephesus was booming. People were joining every Sunday. Timothy had multiple services going on. The church was alive and blossoming.

But by the time second Timothy was written, the situation had changed drastically. Nero had become the Roman Emperor. Nero Claudius Caesar was known for his debaucheries, political murders, and persecution of Christians. He was a lover of music and rumor had it that Nero "fiddled" while Rome burned during the great fire of 64 A.D. Nero was known for his "loose-living", he was known for "stepping on" his political rivals, and he was known for assaulting and insulting those who stood for the liberating gospel of Christ. This political climate created an upstream situation for Timothy. The tactics of Nero were meant to scare believers out of their faith. Some members of the church started leaving the church to save their lives. Attendance in the church of Ephesus started declining.

That was outside of the church. Inside of the church, Timothy had to deal with rebellion among members of his church leadership. Timothy had written a letter to Paul complaining about this. The Epistle of 2 Timothy is Paul's response to what Timothy is going through. No wonder in 2 Timothy Paul says, "Be not therefore ashamed of the testimony of our Lord, nor of me his prisoner: but be a partaker of the afflictions of the gospel according to the power of God." No wonder in 2 Timothy Paul says, "Thou therefore endure hardness, as a good soldier of Jesus Christ." And no wonder Paul says in this letter, "Preach the Word, be ready in season and out of season." Timothy had gone through the "in season" season of ministry when things were going well for him in his church. But the seasons changed! Seasons of ministry do change! Seasons change! People change! Money changes. Regardless of your homiletical prowess, seasons do change! In either season, Paul admonishes Timothy to stay at his post.

"In season and out of season" can refer to external circumstances, but it can also refer to internal disposition. Oswald Chambers has a different read on "in season and out of season". He says "in season and out of season" has to do more with how we feel than with the volatility of external circumstances. "In season" is a time of high inspiration. "Out of season" is a time of low inspiration. Chambers says that Paul is calling us to stay at our posts in seasons of high inspiration and seasons of low inspiration. There are times when you feel it and times when you do not feel it. In either season stay at your post! The temptation for us is to make a god out of inspiration. Inspiration comes and goes. You feel it some Sundays, and some Sundays you do not. If you base your faithfulness on inspiration, you will be present sometimes and other times you will not. We do not walk by inspiration; we walk by faith. Even when the inspiration is not there, do it anyway. Preach by faith not by sight! Inspiration is a nice caboose on the train, but it should not be the engine. Faith is the engine!

To those who are called to preach upstream, Paul declares what we are to do; how we are to do it, and then he tells us **why we are to do it**. Preach the word in light of some facts. Be ready in season out of season with something in your view. Keep some truths in view. What we are to keep in view is implied in v.1. The only way to consistently preach upstream is to do it with the *judgement of Christ in mind*. "I charge you before God and the Lord Jesus Christ, who will judge the…" Judgment in this context has to do with the testing of the integrity of your work. This is not about salvation. Paul says to Timothy your work will be tested one day. In that day the verdict and criticism of people will not matter. The volume of the "Amens" you got in your preaching moments will not matter, because the audience you really want to please is the One who called you. Recognition of this would save us from the touchy spirit which is offended by criticism. Recognition of this would save us from the self-important spirit which is concerned with personal rights and personal prestige. Recognition of this would save us from the self-centered spirit which demands thanks and praise. The only critique that really matters emanates from the one who is able to say, "Well done!" "Stop waiting for applause from people who have no hands", says Dr. John Gunns.

The only way to consistently preach upstream is do it with the **appearance of Christ in view**. "...who will judge the living and dead at his appearing." "Appearing" was the word used for the visit of an emperor in a particular city. Knowledge that the emperor is coming is motivation to get and keep things in order! When the emperor was coming, soldiers made sure they were at their post. Preach with this fact in view: Christ is going to appear. His appearance is motivation in itself, because in order for him to appear means he had to overcome some things. Appearance means resurrection.

Resurrection means death could not hold him! His overcoming of death means we are more than conquerors. Resurrection is "being that ain't supposed to be!"

If we are going to preach upstream, we do it with the judgment of Christ in view. We do it with the appearance of Christ in view, and we also do it with the **kingdom of Christ in view**. Why do we preach upstream? We preach upstream because the Lord is our audience and critic; we preach upstream because the Lord will appear, and his appearance implies victory; we preach upstream because the Lord reigns! One of the reasons Timothy may have been discouraged is that he had the wrong face in view. Nero was such a dominant figure that he may have been preaching with the face of the reigning emperor in view. Nero's face was plastered all over FOX news and CNN. Paul needs him to shift his focus. There is one whose kingdom would last forever. Nero reigned for 14 years. I am not sure how long "Nero" will reign in our times. But our Lord reigns forever! Keep your eye on him. Our youth Choir sang recently and there was a little girl in the first row of the choir stands who I thought

Chapter One

was looking at me when she was singing. I was seated on the front row of the church, and I was feeling some pride because it looked like the little girl was looking at her pastor for inspiration. I was just waving and smiling. But then I noticed the little girl was moving her head around as though she was trying to see around me. When I turned around, I noticed that her father was directly behind me. I moved to the side and noticed that the girl's face brightened up and she started "sangin" for real. I was in her way. She needed to sing with her father in view. Get some of the distractions out of your view. Preach with the reigning King in view.

Preach upstream! The salmon do all they can to get upstream. They do it because they want to reproduce more salmon. The work involved in getting upstream costs adult salmon their lives. Most of them die off after eggs have been produced and more salmon are reproduced. The only way for us to make disciples, the only way to reproduce citizens of the kingdom is for us to make the sacrifice of preaching and ministering upstream!

Chapter Two

No More Home Field Advantage

One of the things that sports teams fight for in their pursuit of championships is something called "home field or home court advantage." When the regular season is over and teams get to the "postseason", they want to know that they will be playing in front of hospitable fans for the majority of their games. These teams understand that what they do on the court or field is influenced by the support they have in the stands. What they do in each case will be easier if the majority of the people in the stands are on their side. Teams that are not playing on their home court or field know from the outset that they have an extra hurdle to overcome in accomplishing their objectives.

I recently heard Christian author, professor, theologian, cultural guru, Leonard Sweet say that "Christianity now plays all away games, we no longer have home field or home court advantage." Christianity, or at least some form of it, used to have home court and field advantage in America. It no longer does. We are playing on someone else's court. The fans in the stands are no longer hospitable to matters of faith. Matters of faith, church mores, practices, and theology used to have an extreme home court advantage in the Black community. Even people who did not attend church would at least welcome the message and the ways of faith. Almost everyone in Black families had at least been exposed to ecclesiastical customs and to the gospel of Jesus Christ. For the most part, Black folks lived with a religious sub-stratum that made us amenable to things of faith. No longer is this the case.

The current cultural belief is that life can be lived,

reality can be created, and battles can be fought without God being a key player. God has become a relic of the past. The truth is, we started losing home court advantage around the middle of the 17th century when Copernicus challenged the Ptolemaic notion that the earth was the center of the universe. The new heliocentric theory that the sun was the center of the universe elevated science and mechanical physics. Christianity suffered a major blow because the universe was no longer seen as the field of arbitrary divine action, but as an interpretable realm of law. In other words, science began to push faith out of the way. Copernicus caused us to lose home court advantage!

Not only can we blame Copernicus we can also put some blame on the philosopher, Rene Descartes. Descartes promulgated the idea that all knowledge was subject to question unless it was beyond all doubt; that all conceptions must be doubted until proven and they must have the certainty of mathematical demonstration. In other words, if it's not empirically verifiable, "it ain't true." Belief in God was a casualty of this philosophical system. The irony is that both Copernicus and Descartes were devout Catholics. They probably had no clue as to how their theories would hasten the move toward a secularized mindset and subsequently cause us to lose home court advantage. We thought we had the advantage after the Reformation, but such was not the case. Two of our own people gave our home court advantage away.

The bottom-line is that we are living in a world where God is not seen as a key player. Charles Taylor says that our world suffers from the disease of the "malaise of immanence." Our world has been freed from the reality of transcendence and enchantment. There appears to be no transcendent point of reference. God has been pushed out of the picture. Walter Brueggemann refers to this phenomenon as the "dethroning of Christian privilege." Because we no longer have home court advantage, we cannot look to the stands for support. "There was a time… when the Christian preacher could count on the shared premises of the listening community…" The listening community no longer has shared premises. Everyone comes with their own set of ideas and beliefs. Churches are populated by people determined to live out their own truths.

Chapter Two

In the seventeenth century, it was hard work to imagine a world without God. And now, in the 21st century, it is hard to imagine the world with God.

We now pastor in the midst of atheists; and to some extent we pastor atheists. That may seem a bit hyperbolic, but maybe not. Our churches and our communities are not inhabited by confessional atheists. Confessional atheists verbally declare that they do not believe in God. Practical atheists never declare that they do not believe in God. As a matter of fact, practical atheists actually say that they believe in God. They affirm their belief in God and Christ in creedal formulae. However, they never make a connection between creed believed and life lived. Psalm 14:1 is very interesting. It says, "The fool hath said in his/her [emphasis added] heart, 'There is no God'... they have done abominable works..." (KJV). Fools may not say it with their mouths, but they say it in their hearts. For the Hebrew, the heart was the center of being. Fools do not have room for God in the center of their being. Practical atheism may affirm the existence of God, but it does not see God as a key player in living. Practical atheism makes no connection between God and justice. Practical atheism makes no connection between God and sexuality and gender identity. Practical atheism makes no connection between God and racism. Practical atheism makes no connection between God and militarism. **When there is no connection between God and the arenas of human living, the result will be chaos and confusion. When there is no connection between God and the arenas of human living, the result will be an inversion of right and wrong.**

New gods abound in the land. I'm in agreement with New York University academic, Scott Galloway who contends that we have four relatively new gods in our society: Google, Apple, Facebook, and Amazon. Google is the god of omniscience that knows everything. Where people used to turn to religion for answers, now we turn to Google. Google is now being asked to answer questions of deep human meaning.

Apple is viewed as the god and goddess of sex. To have an iPhone, says Galloway, is a sign of success and influence and it acts as a mating signal. For some of our young people, the iPhone is an extension of themselves. It adds or takes away from their attractiveness.

Facebook is the god of love. Facebook is used to connect with friends, relatives, and acquaintances. In many cases, through likes and shares, it keeps a barometer of how loved and popular we are.

Amazon is the god of omnipresence and omnipotence. Whatever you need it can get it to you wherever you are and as quickly as you need it. There is a new pantheon of gods that have contributed to our loss of the home court advantage.

What are we to do as the church? How is the church empowered in this kind of climate? The very God we preach is now viewed as unnecessary. The preacher is seen as a VCR vendor; cute and sentimental, but obsolete. All of our games are away games. What are we to do? We are dispensers of God's Word, but no one seems to want this God. What's our recourse? There are no easy answers to this complex conundrum, however, there are some things for us to consider.

Paul was in a similar situation. He happened to be hanging around Athens while waiting for Silas and Timothy to come hang out with him. He was not on his home court. While there, he noticed that the city was full of idols. Jerusalem was the ancient city of religion. Rome was the ancient city of politics and power. Athens was the city of philosophy and academic pursuits. It was full of idols and Paul noticed it. Paul walked up and down the streets of Athens noticing the busts of certain deities in people's yards. He noticed the idols because he simply paid attention. As preachers, part of our calling is to simply pay attention to what is happening around us and whose home court we are on. Some time ago, I was on a United Airlines flight leaving the Atlanta area. As we were ascending, the plane was being tossed around by the turbulence. It was a bumpy climb to the desired altitude. While all of that was going on around us, the flight attendants continued giving their usual greeting and speech. Sprinkled throughout the opening greetings was the repetition of United's tagline, "Welcome to the friendly skies." The skies were anything but friendly, and there was nothing said that indicated the attendants knew what was going on around us.

Chapter Two

Part of our ministry is to just look and notice. Over half of the people who attend Calvary church in Morristown New Jersey do not live in Morristown. They commute from various counties and even from Pennsylvania and New York. I am grateful for them and appreciate the effort they make to get to church. But sometimes I'm afraid that they simply come in and go home after church without ever noticing what's really happening in our surrounding community. I'm not sure if they notice the changing demographic. I'm not sure if they notice that the number of Black businesses has dwindled down to almost nothing. I'm not sure if they notice that churches were the last institutions to fully reopen after the height of the pandemic. The only way that Paul was able to see that Athens was full of idols was because he paid attention!

First, to do fruitful ministry on the opposition's home court requires noticing what is going on around us. It also requires *presenting an alternative*. After noticing the idols, Paul then goes to the synagogue, the marketplace, and the Areopagus. He goes to the church, he goes to the business sector, and he goes to the halls of academia to present an alternative. The alternative was the gospel. He is not on his home court, but he is confident enough in the gospel that he is willing to take it anywhere. We have an alternative to the opposition, and it will travel. The gospel does not need the advantage of home court or field. Jesus was not on his home field when he cast out the legion of demons from the demoniac of Gadara. Jesus was not on his home field when he said in Mark 4:39, "Peace be still." to the contrary winds of adversity. Jesus was not on his home field when he descended into hell and preached to the spirits. We have an alternative about which we do not need to be sheepish or embarrassed. I'm confident that the gospel can stand on its own two feet in the synagogue, in the marketplace, and in the Areopagus.

I agree with Brueggemann that, "The church has a job. The preacher has the job of inviting the community to reimagine the world as though Yahweh were a key and decisive player." In this sense, preaching and ministry are "subversive". Brueggemann is correct to say that "preaching is never the dominant version." Ministry and preaching are always a version, a rendering of reality that lives under the dominant version. The dominant version is one in which God is not seen as a key player. The sub-version is that without God I could do nothing. Without Him I would fail. Without the Lord my life would be rugged, like a ship without a sail.

In an effort to reach the surrounding culture we do not need to replicate it. We offer the alternative, and we need to be confident in the alternative we offer. There is nothing wrong with being innovative in ministry, but we do not have to succumb to the temptation of being trendy. There is a difference between being innovative and being trendy. To be innovative means to be daring and creative in implementing fresh technique and cutting-edge programming. To be trendy means to assimilate to what everyone else is doing around you in order to appear to be progressive. To be trendy is to try whatever seems to be "trending" even if it does not fit your context. Even though we do not have the home court advantage, we do not have to replicate and duplicate the surrounding culture. There's nothing wrong with "church" life being different than the rest of life. It's alright if our worship spaces look like churches. It's alright if clergy look like clergy. It's alright if we sing "All Hail the Power of Jesus' Name." It's alright if our sermons include references to the cross and to heaven. We do not have to dumb down in order to reach out! It's ok for us to be strange. There is nothing odd about the church maintaining its "oddity." Resist the temptation to secularize preaching. Keep God in the center of it instead of human aggrandizement!

Paul was confident enough in the alternative to present it without apology. We have something that we can lovingly declare in our messaging and in our loving of people that will work even if we are not on our home turf. The gospel always works. Love always works. Service always works. Sacrifice always works.

If we are going to do fruitful ministry on someone else's home turf it may mean *going back further in our messaging*. When Paul finally gets a hearing in front of the Council of the Areopagus, he begins by talking about where they are with the gods they serve. He had seen altars with inscriptions to the "unknown god." Paul takes his message back, further than he typically would, in order to connect with where they were. When

Paul preached in Antioch, he went as far back as Egypt and Canaan in his preaching because that's what that audience understood. When Paul preached in Thessalonica, he went as far back as preaching the necessity of the Messiah suffering, because they had a conception of the Messiah. When Paul preached at Ephesus, he talked to them about receiving the Holy Spirit, because that's where they were in their understanding. In all of these places, the church had some semblance of home court advantage. But here in Athens, Paul was playing an away game, therefore he had to take his message even farther back, because the people of Athens had no previous understanding of the gospels.

Christian privilege has been dethroned in our current setting, therefore our preaching, theology, and ministry may have to start farther back. Our listeners, to some degree, have learned to construe the real practice of their lives without reference to the claims of God. When I grew up, I was not exposed to Judaism or Islam. The only thing I had been exposed to was "all things Christian." Therefore, when my pastor preached, he did not have to go beyond John 3:16. When my children grew up, they had friends who were

Jewish and Muslim. We had to take preaching and teaching to them farther back because their Christian worldview had been exposed to other worldviews. We did not need our Sunday School teachers to talk to us about why Jesus was THE way to salvation. We just assumed that Jesus is. Because of the dethroning of Christian privilege, today's Sunday School teachers may have to go farther back to find a different starting point for teaching. When my children grew up, they only saw "male and female" romantic interaction on television. That is not the case for my grandchildren. Therefore, with them I may not be able to begin with a simple explanation of the so-called "birds and bees."

Paul goes farther back in his preaching and teaching, and he ends up at a destination point where all of us should end up in our preaching and teaching. He starts off with the "unknown gods", but he ends up talking about the One who has been raised from the dead. When we are not on our home courts, we may have to find different starting points in our ministries and preaching, but we should end up at the same place. All roads lead to the empty tomb.

Chapter Two

Sometimes we criticize the old, Black preacher for always closing his sermons with the cross and resurrection. But maybe that's not such a bad practice. Charles Spurgeon once said to his students at Preacher's College, "Gentlemen, wherever you start your sermon, make way as rapidly as you can across country to Calvary." Gardner Taylor reminds us that Calvary is our central theme. He says, "Don't let the devil drive you from our central place..." Calvary is the place where God got underneath all that was wrong with the world, turned it upside down in order to turn it right side up. Calvary was the place where God met the enemy head on and turned him back. Calvary was the place where God did all that needed to be done, once and for all, forever. And the last cry that issues up from Calvary is not the cry of a defeated soul. It is the exultant shout of our victorious Savior as he mounts red altar steps toward his coronation. This is the message that will work home court advantage, or no home court advantage.

Chapter Three

Reimagining Expository Preaching

A Personal Pilgrimage

There was always something about preaching that resonated with me. Even when I was a neophyte in the faith, I gravitated toward this enterprise called "preaching." However, I attempted to conceal this hidden attraction I had to preaching. I was young. I was sixteen years old when I started feeling something. I didn't necessarily feel a call to preach at that age, but I did sense a subtle "pull" and "tug". There were times when I would sneak and listen to some of my dad's preaching records. We had "33's" back then. I would go back into his room when he left the house and listen to C.L. Franklin's "The Eagle Stirreth Her Nest." I recall listening to Leo Daniels' sermon "Let Your Hair Down." There were other records and eventually cassettes I would listen to during my high school years.

Between listening to these records and cassettes and hearing my dad, Jerry Carter Sr., preach on Sunday mornings, I was exposed to an abundance of "narrative preaching." The imagination of the black preacher in those days gripped me. To hear C.L. Franklin masterfully tell the story and develop the metaphor of the construction of the eagle's nest and the process of expelling those young eaglets from the nest sold me on this narrative approach. To hear my father recount the prodigal son's steps back to his father's house was mesmerizing. There were many black preachers who had not had the opportunity to go to college or seminary. The technical skills of homiletics were not developed in many of them. Therefore, the one thing they had to nurture was "imagination." They were doing narrative preaching long before narrative preaching became popularized by the dominant culture and western seminaries. Narrative preaching is to the homiletical world what collard greens and kale greens are to the culinary world. All of a sudden fancy restaurants are serving collards and kale as though they are new vegetables. Our folks have been eating that stuff a long time. Narrative preaching has been referred to as the "new homiletic" in some predominantly white seminaries. There's nothing "new" about narrative preaching.

In any event I was exposed to that approach to preaching as a boy. I liked preaching but I didn't want to preach. It was what my father did. I didn't want to do it, primarily because of my desire to rebel against my expected and predicted pathway. It was my desire to play college football and pursue a law degree. But in January of 1983 I felt an overwhelming summons to preach the gospel while I sat in the Mt. Period Baptist church of Columbus, Ohio as my father preached on the marks of a Christian from Galatians chapter 6. I went through the process and on July 24, 1983, I preached my initial/trial sermon entitled "You

Must be Born Again." In January of 1984 my father took me to the National Baptist board meeting in Nashville, Tn. It was there where I heard A. Louis Patterson for the first time, and it changed my thinking about preaching. He preached from the parable of the "Good Samaritan." It was the first time that I was exposed to "expository preaching." He didn't just tell the story, he broke it up into "chunks", or "points", or "moves." I remember his outline. He said this certain Samaritan provided, "instantaneous relief, insightful referral, immediate resources, and finally promised an imminent return." That idea floored me.

I was sold immediately. I have held on to Patterson's sermon and outline until this point. I found out that narrative preaching was not the only way to preach, but that there were other ways that are just as effective. However, there was something about that expository sermon that changed my thinking about preaching. Each June after that I attended the National Baptist congress in various cities. I would hear Caesar Clark in the morning along with Manuel Scott, Sr.

I would hear Scott again in the afternoon along with A. Louis Patterson. Those years of hearing

Chapter Three

Patterson shaped my approach to the preaching assignment. I started ascribing to expository preaching without even knowing what it was. This homiletical slant was strengthened in March of 1987 when I was exposed to the preaching of the late E.K. Bailey. I heard him preaching "Stilling the Storm" in Columbus, Ohio. Based on Mark 4:35-41, Bailey's sermon was framed by three moves: the journey of the ship, the severity of the storm, and the mastery of the Savior.

Exposure to both Patterson and Bailey brought some structure to the narrative approach formed in me from my childhood. I started looking for outlines in sermons, and I began using alliteration in my sermonic moves. Alliteration proved to be a good memory aid for the hearer and an artistic expression of my preaching. Since those early days of my preaching journey, I have experienced several other sermonic influences, and my preaching has gone through several evolutionary stages (and is still evolving for that matter). The heart of it, however, is still this bent toward "exposition."

An Understanding of Expository Preaching

What is expository preaching? It's like good music; it is hard to define. You just know it when you hear it. Expository preaching is both a philosophy and a form of preaching. It is a broad philosophy of preaching that sees scripture as the starting point of the sermon. The starting point of the sermon is not a topic from a current event or a life experience. The starting point of the sermon is not some experience in nature. Topics from the news, life experiences, truths from literature or the arts, and observations from nature may trigger a sermonic thought, but thought is quickly tied to the written Word of God. The starting point of the sermon is the passage of scripture itself.

As a philosophy, expository preaching anchors in the authority of scripture. This is not a technical authority that focuses on biblical inerrancy. It is an authority that is founded on the function of the scripture. At the heart of the expository approach is a belief that God gives birth to what God desires through the Word. Whatever God desires, God says, "Let there be…", and whatever is announced in the "Let there be…" comes to pass. So, if God desires for light to be created, God does not have to work to produce light. God just says, "Let there be light." Electricity is seen as something that was discovered by the likes of Benjamin Franklin and so on. God did not "discover" light, he created it by his Word. In the words of Gardner Taylor, "When God says let there be, all non-being has to give way to being." That happens because of the Word. The Word gives birth to what is in the mind of God. When Jesus desires to exorcise demons out of the man in the synagogue, all Jesus has to do is announce it with His Word. He tells the demons to "come out." And what he announces accomplishes what he desires. At the bottom of the expository approach is a belief in the authority of scripture. It is an authority that accomplishes what God desires.

Most of the time when we speak of expository preaching in preaching circles, we refer to it as a form of preaching. In the first instance exposition is a general philosophy. In the second case it is a form of preaching. This form of preaching has been particularly attractive to some African American preachers because of the black preacher's affinity for biblical preaching.

Cleophus Larue, in *The Heart of Black Preaching*, identifies the distinctives of black preaching. The first one he identifies is preaching that has a strong biblical content. Larue contends that:

> In many black churches, biblical preaching, defined as preaching that allows a text from the bible to serve as the leading force in shaping the content and purpose of the sermon, is the type of preaching considered to be most faithful to traditional understandings of the proclaimed word.

An expository sermon, in the words of Bryan Chapell, "may be defined as a message whose structure and thought are derived from a biblical text, that covers the scope of the text, and that explains the features and context of the text in order to disclose the enduring principles for faithful thinking, living and worship intended by the Spirit, who inspired the text." The primary take away from Chapell's definition is that in expository preaching the biblical text shapes the thought and structure of the sermon.

H. Grady Davis goes a little further. For him the idea, the substance and the form of the sermon are all born of the biblical text. Exposition says

Chapter Three

that you do not abandon the text after you have gleaned your idea and gathered your substance. The form of the sermon is determined by the contours of the text itself. The biblical passage determines your moves. Effective sermons need both substance and shape. Some sermons have solid substance but no shape; others have organized and sequential shape and form but little substance.

The expository sermon views the scriptural text as both source and resource. Scripture gives birth to the sermon, and it directs the sermon along the way. Exposition does not abandon the text along the way, having simply used the text as a starting point. Therefore, grammar is essential. The tense of verbs is critical. And, central to the passage, is the meaning of its words. The expository sermon allows for a scripture like Philippians 4:7 to be read purposefully: "And the peace of God, which transcends all understanding, will GUARD your hearts and minds...." Exposition pays attention to the fact that "guard" is a military word which means "to garrison around." It carries the idea of protecting in the midst of a heated battle.

Expository preaching is typically well-organized and sequential. It works its way, in a linear fashion, toward a conclusion. The question is, "Does expository preaching still work"? In congregations where hearers are drawn to storytelling, does this linear approach to preaching still have a place? Cicero said that the orator has three duties: "to prove (probare); to delight (delectate); and to stir or move (flectare). Probare is to stimulate the mind; delectate is to speak to the emotions; and flectare is to move the will to decision making. To some extent, the job of the preacher is the same. The question is, "Can expository preaching do that?" My contention is that this preaching form still has a place and can still move the hearer; however, we need to rethink it in light of what Jesus models in Luke 24.

In this chapter, two disciples are brought back from the brink of disillusionment to the horizon of joy all because of the ministry of Jesus. Jesus' activity and approach in this passage is a paradigm for contemporary exposition.

Jesus' ministry is characterized by CONTEXTUALIZATION. It is Easter evening. As is typical, pilgrims return home the Sunday after

Chapter Three

Passover. Two of them are headed to some obscure village called Emmaus. As they are engaging in their mobile pity-party, Jesus joins them. He journeys with them in order to find out where they are emotionally and spiritually. Jesus does not immediately reveal his identity. And they don't pick up on it because they have become secure, resting in their unbelief. They have anchored in sorrow and sadness.

Jesus walks with them long enough to give them a chance to articulate their hopelessness and unbelief. He does not immediately judge them for where they are in their journey, He simply joins them. Unless he does this, he will not be able to determine a starting point for his preaching.

Expository preaching reimagined is preaching that walks with people on their shattered journeys and pilgrimages. Exposition cannot ignore the plights of the people to whom it preaches. Although the starting point of the sermon is scripture, the preacher has to be aware of what is happening on the Emmaus Road. It becomes easy to hide out in the passage of scripture, so as to find refuge from the stormy blast of societal context. The temptation is to hide out in scripture without a working knowledge of the Emmaus

Road experience. Some expository preachers hide out in the bible! When the expository preacher ignores the racism, the institutional discrimination, the fear, the natural disasters of the Emmaus Road, he or she becomes irrelevant. Joseph Sizoo, in his book *Preaching Unashamed*, said that a preacher must know at least four things, namely "his times, her Bible, his gospel, and himself/herself." Attentiveness to social context and social location demands that expository preaching have a prophetic slant to it.

As I'm writing this, I get a call from the hospital that one of our members is in critical condition. The temptation is to stay in the office and work with this text, but there are family members on the Emmaus Road whom I may need to join on their pilgrimage. I am literally picking up where I left off before I got the call. I spent time with them on the Emmaus Road of terrible grief as we all stood there and watched this sister die right in front of us. Having walked down the road with them, having heard them question God, having heard them crying in anguish, I now know what it is in scripture they may need to hear. Expository preaching of our times must take into account

Chapter Three

the reality of the historical, economic, political, technological, environmental and existential context in which it occurs.

Expository preaching, according to this narrative, takes into account contextualization, and also has a continued focus on EXPLANATION. After revealing himself to the two disciples Jesus then explains the scriptures. The "explaining" is in the imperfect tense, which means that Jesus had been explaining as a process. He took his time and worked through the scriptures. He explains to them what was said. Expository preaching, even reimagined, "says what has been said." Expository preaching exposes. "Expositio" (in Latin) means to "set forth." The expositor "sets forth" what is in the passage. He or she exposes what has been said. Exposition mines a passage of scripture for all that is there; it doesn't jump around from text to text. The expository sermon rebels against the "butterfly sermon." The "butterfly sermon", in the words of Lloyd Perry, "flits from book to book not lighting too long at any spot lest someone should catch him!"

After Jesus has spent some Emmaus Road time with them, he is able to explain the scriptures in light of what he has found out about these disciples. If he engages in explanation without having connected to contextualization he would be "scratching where they're not itching." Discoveries in contextualization help to shape scriptural explanation. I had a recent conversation with my oldest son about why he chooses to stream Sunday morning worship instead of attending physically. I spent that time with him on the Emmaus Road and it may help to shape some of my explanation of scripture to him and to other millennials, because I've found out why there is more of a comfort with him staying at home.

Explanation works with what has been given. Ramesh Richard, in the opening lines of his work on expository preaching, says that he had a conversation with a Nigerian sculptor who had made many wood sculptures. The sculptor said to him, "The tree is what God made; the sculpture is what I make with what god has made." The text is what God makes; the sermon is what we make out of what God has made. The passage is given to us! What do we do with it? Jesus explains what is there.

Chapter Three

Explanation says what has been said, explanation always views Christ as the "ends" of what it says. The expository form of preaching, as other forms of Christian preaching, aims at Christ as the "ends" of the sermon. It is not clear which scriptures Jesus explains. However, it doesn't matter because all of them point to him. Jesus is both the preacher and the content of the sermon in this passage. The job of the expositor is to ultimately present Christ. Ian MacPherson has charged us "to preach Christ evangelically, as Savior and Lord; to preach Christ ethically, as Teacher and Example; and to preach Christ eschatologically as destined Judge and Ruler of the world." Whenever we explain the scriptures, the explanation should end with an evangelical, ethical, or eschatological glimpse of the Carpenter from Nazareth.

Expository preaching reimagined sees the importance of contextualization, anchors in explanation, and enhances explanation with ILLUSTRATION. After explaining the scripture, the incognito Christ attempts to leave. The two disciples are inching their way toward revelation of who Jesus is, but they are not quite there. They strongly urge him to stay. He stays with them, and while they are at the table Jesus takes bread, gives thanks, breaks it and gives it to them. Jesus, who is their guest, now acts as host. Jesus does not force his way in. He stands and knocks. But once he is allowed to come in, Jesus takes over. He is known for that. Once you let him in, he will take over.

The breaking of the bread, which may be a communion or Eucharistic type of meal, is reminiscent of the upper room experience. Fred Craddock says there are three ways to experience an event: "in its rehearsal; in its reality; and in its remembrance." For a wedding there is a wedding rehearsal, the actual wedding, and anniversaries in which the wedding is remembered. The upper room was the experience of Jesus' death in rehearsal. The first breaking of the bread and sharing of the cup anticipated what was about to happen on that Friday. The reality occurred on that Friday when he hung between earth and heaven. The remembrance is what happens every time we gather around the table.

Something happens in the breaking of the bread. These disciples remember something. Their eyes are opened, and they recognize him. **The**

breaking of the bread is an ocular illustration that buttresses the explanation. Illustration helps to make explanation plain. Their eyes are opened because of an illustration that helps to ameliorate the sullen insensitivity of the two disciples. Expository preaching needs a verbal or visual illustration to make it plain. Illustrations add seasoning to plain and insipid points and propositions.

Expository preaching, reimagined, invests in contextualization, engages in explanation, sees the need for illustration, and aims at TRANSFORMATION. This is not contextualization for the sake of just sounding relevant. This is not explanation for the sake of impressing. I've heard expositors who sometimes give these long dissertations on the Greek and Hebrew with the aim of ostentatiously parading knowledge. This is not illustration for the sake of titillating the senses of the hearer. The aim is transformation. The condition of the disciples on the Emmaus Road is too critical for us to be cute and impressive. Who knows where these two would have ended up had it not been for a faithful "expositor" like Jesus?

As a result of the ministry of Christ, these disciples end up being transformed. What does transformation look like for them? It looks like eyes that are opened; hearts that are burning; and feet that are walking. Eyes that are opened, that is illumination; hearts that are burning, that is a change in disposition; feet that are walking, that is participation. Their eyes are opened. There are some things they see differently. Their hearts are burning. Listen to their testimony: "Were not our hearts burning… as he was talking…and opening." All of the verbs are imperfect participles which means that this was a process. There is no immediate opening of the eyes, burning of the heart, or walking of the feet. It happens as the scriptures are being opened up. The scriptures are opened up first, so that eyes can be opened up. The expositor has to be patient with blind people whose feet are now walking. These same disciples who were headed toward Emmaus were not redirected; they end up heading back to Jerusalem. They head back to the place that was the source of their sorrow. But now they head back with a message, because there are still people caught in the grip of what they were caught in. They go back to participate in a hopeless world to be witnesses to the truth!

Chapter Three

The faithful preaching of the Word leads to the opening of the eyes, which means a change in how people think. It leads to a burning of the heart, which means a change in how people feel. And it leads to walking feet, which means a change in what people do. This Word is meant to do more than wreck the house. This Word is meant to do more than just get people to more revivals. This Word is meant to do more than illicit a cheap thrill. This Word is meant to change the plight of those who are on their Emmaus Road through faithful exposition.

Chapter Four

Magnetic Preaching

I once heard Dr. Anthony Campolo tell of a group of people who went on a tour of a popular oil refinery. The tour guide showed them where and how the crude oil is transformed into gasoline and diesel fuel. The refinery tour guide explained to them that the refining process included, "separation, conversion, and treatment." They were then shown the intricate machinery used in this tedious process. At the end of the tour, one of the tourists raised the questions: "Where is the shipping department? Where is the area where what you produce is sent out into the world?" The tour guide, who was a representative of the company, embarrassingly and nervously replied, "There is no shipping department, everything we produce is used to keep the refinery going!"

There was no place where what was being produced was being sent out to the world beyond the refinery. I wonder, if that is the case with our preaching and ministry? In the quietness of my own praying and thinking ground, I ask myself if there is a shipping department in my preaching, or if most of my preaching is aimed at keeping the institution going. Each week, like many of you, through the power of the Spirit, I go through the process of transforming the crude oil of biblical texts into the gasoline of sermonic presentations. After the process of separation, conversion and treatment is complete, what then? Are there any dimensions of my preaching that are sent out through the shipping department, or is most of my preaching intended to keep the church and her constituents going?

This question haunts me. It has been hovering over my head like a foreboding cloud for some time now. After wrestling with the question for some time I concluded that most of my preaching is aimed at insiders. I'm troubled with having come to this conclusion, but it is nevertheless true. The ear that I have in mind in sermon preparation, more often than not, is the ear that is already "saved, sanctified, Holy Ghost filled, and fire baptized." I'm probably not alone in this homiletical dilemma. Most of the sermons I hear from colleagues and peers alike seem to be tailored at keeping the refinery going. Perhaps we are more comfortable preaching to the ear of the insider than we are the outsider. It is easier to write sermons for deacons, trustees, and choir members than it is to write for corporate executives, agnostics, and young adults who may have little interest in matters of faith and the institutions connected to matters of faith.

Kanye West and Jay-Z lyrically and poetically put it like this in their hit "No Church in the Wild": "Human beings in a mob, What's a mob to a king? What's a God to a non-believer who don't believe in anything? Will he make it out alive? Alright, alright, No church in the wild." In this song, Kanye and Jay-Z claim that there is no church in the wild. I wonder if that is true. Is the gospel that I preach a gospel for the wild as well as for the domesticated masses of the congregations?

Writing and preaching sermons for the insider, the "churched", and the saved ear is just easier and honestly, more enjoyable than writing and preaching for the outsider, unchurched, unsaved ear. The "Amens of affirmation" are more bountiful when I'm aiming at the insider's ear. I can be "deep and theologically sophisticated" when I'm preaching for the insider. It appears that we are more interested in writing and preaching sermons that will please the insider, because our aim is to "kill the house" and to be applauded for having done so. I was driving the late Dr. Mack King Carter around once and he said to me, "Jerry, most preachers are more interested in sermonizing than they are proclaiming the kerygma."

It appears as though Evangelistic preaching is too basic and elementary. It is frighteningly ordinary. In the words of D.T. Niles, it is simply "one beggar telling another beggar where to find bread." Evangelistic preaching asserts that the whole of humanity stands in the shoes of the beggar. Some are beggars in rags. Others are beggars in velvet, but are beggars, nonetheless.

Some beggars have PhD's; some beggars have GED's. Evangelistic preaching offers the "wonder" bread of life to beggars who have yet to find it.

Chapter Four

This kind of preaching is not always that exciting. This kind of preaching will not result in premiere preaching platforms, nor will it land you on star-studded sermonic stages.

The academy and the world of homiletics itself doesn't seem to be aligned with preaching to the ear and soul of the outsider as much as it is to the ear and soul of the insider. The study of preaching appears to be more interested, if not exclusively interested, in drawing those who have been drawn instead of those who are a "great distance away." I was looking through one of our seminal and foundational preaching handbooks recently for any articles or information on evangelistic preaching. The handbook is over five hundred pages long. There are long entries in the handbook on literary criticism, preaching social justice, philosophical hermeneutics, feminist and womanist criticism, metalogical preaching, and so on. Amongst these entries were a few pages devoted to the discussion of evangelistic preaching. The academy has outgrown evangelism, often viewing evangelistic preaching as an outdated form of primitive "fire and brimstone" proclamation, relegated to the boundaries of the revivalistic movements which we outgrew centuries ago.

To be sure, our preaching definitely has a role in shaping the lives and faith of insiders. The writer of Ephesians says:

> The gifts he gave were that some would be apostles, some prophets, some evangelists, some pastors and teachers, to equip the saints for the work of ministry, for building up the body of Christ, until all of us come to the unity of the faith and the knowledge of the Son of God, to maturity, to the measure of the full stature of Christ. (Eph. 4:11-13, NRSV)

Preaching is one of God's tools that is used to nurture and develop the life of discipleship. We are called to craft sermons for those who are considered to be insiders. "...faith comes by hearing and hearing by the Word of God" (Romans 10:17, NKJV). Our preaching widens and deepens the faith of those who are already "in."

However, it is my contention that every sermon should at least have a minimal evangelistic appeal. One of the first descriptions of the Christian preacher was not doctor, reverend, bishop, or pastor; it was "fisher of people." Jesus calls us with a view of drawing the outsider in. Embedded in Paul's instruction to Timothy, in response to living and doing ministry in the "last days", was to do the work of an evangelist. The beginning of Luke 15 challenges us to shape our preaching with not just the insider in mind, but the outsider as well. Particularly, the first few verses of this chapter dare us to shape sermons that draw those who dwell in the margins.

"Then drew near unto him all the publicans and sinners for to hear him. And the Pharisees and scribes murmured saying 'this man receiveth sinners and eateth with them.' And he spake this parable saying..." (Luke 15:1-3, KJV). This passage challenges us, in the bedrock of our souls, to *model the magnetic preaching of Jesus.*

"Then drew near unto him all the publicans (tax collectors) to hear him...." Who was being drawn to him? It wasn't the church folks. It wasn't the preachers and pastors. It wasn't the ecclesiastical leadership. It was the tax-collectors and the sinners; the wrong kind of people. Tax-collectors were despised because of their dealings with Rome. They were considered dirty because of their contact with Gentiles. They were considered unclean because they could not observe the cleansing rituals. "Sinners" were despised because of their sins. Who were these "sinners"? I do not know if these so-called sinners were any more sinful than the folks who despised them; it's just that their sin was probably more conspicuous. In both cases these were people who were unable to adhere to all of the Jewish purification practices. They were considered "unclean". These were the people who would not normally be in the company of religious folks. There was nothing about "church" that drew them. Jesus, who is always one step ahead of his church, had a ministry which attracted the "wrong type" of people.

They were drawn to Jesus. They didn't just decide to come to Jesus. I appreciate the language of the ancient King James Version. They were drawn to him. It was almost an unconscious attraction. The reason many of us are connected to Christ today is because he "drew" us. We didn't just decide to make Jesus our choice. He drew us. Jesus said, "No one can come to Me unless the Father who sent Me draws them" (Jn. 6:44, NKJV). The reason it took being drawn was because some of us were so immobilized and trapped,

Chapter Four

that it required a force to pull us out. The pull is irresistible. As he draws us, we come to him.

"Then drew near unto him all the publicans and sinners..." What was it that drew them? The clue is in the first line. The sinners and tax-collectors gathered around him to hear him. If they gathered around him to hear him, whatever drew them had something to do with what he was saying. In some cases, it was the performance of miracles that drew people. But Jesus never really performed miracles to draw a crowd. In this case, it wasn't the miracles that drew them; it was what he was preaching that was magnetic.

There was something about what he was saying that drew this particular demographic. The kind of message that Jesus proclaimed, and the kind of ministry he embodied was modeled in the preceding chapter. The beginning of chapter 15 says, "Then drew near..." Then is an adverb which indicates a connection to timing. What was he preaching and modeling in chapter 14? He was preaching a message that **prioritized transformation**. In this chapter Jesus heals a man on the Sabbath. The Pharisees criticize Jesus for that. Jesus informs them that changing that life was more important than honoring a code. Jesus preached a gospel that put lives before laws. "Then drew near sinners..."

Also in chapter 14, Jesus preached a message that **embodied inclusion**. In verse 12 Jesus said, when you have dinner, don't just invite people who can invite you back. Include those who are at the bottom of the caste system and have no resources to feed you. Include them in the party! "Then drew near sinners..."

In chapter 14 Jesus preached a message that **announced salvation**. He spoke a parable that said that everything is now ready, go to the highways and tell people to come to the table. There is nothing they have to bring. Grace has provided everything that is necessary. Anything that humanity adds to what has been prepared will do nothing but mess it up! "Then drew near sinners..."

What did he preach? He preached a message that **accentuated radical discipleship**. To a multitude of seekers, in verse 27 Jesus said, "And whoever does not bear the cross, and come after Me, cannot be My disciple." This was

Chapter Four

Jesus' message to seekers. He did not hide the demands of the gospel in order to draw a crowd. Craig Loscalzo says that "We are hucksters of cheap grace if we peddle a gospel bereft of demands." Jesus promulgated the demands of the gospel. "Then drew near sinners..." The last thing Jesus says in chapter 14 is "Whoever has ears to hear, let them hear." His message was a whosoever will message. The only prerequisite was that you had to have ears to hear. Chapter 15 begins by identifying the "whoever" as sinners and publicans. Jesus' preaching was magnetic, and evidently, these sinners and publicans had ears to hear.

What shocks me about this text is the kind of people Jesus attracts. He attracts people who seem to be the most opposite from himself. He is so holy; the publicans and sinners are so unholy. Yet, scientifically, that's how magnetism works. A magnet is any object that has a magnetic field. The magnetic field is the space surrounding the magnet which attracts what is opposite of the magnet. Similar magnetic poles repel each other. Different poles attract each other. "Opposites attract" is actually a cliché which is rooted in the world of physics. Jesus' holiness attracts the sinners because they are so in touch with their unholiness that it makes them the opposite of what Jesus is, and therefore there is an attraction. The reason the Pharisees are not attracted to Jesus is because they think they too are holy, which makes them think they are like Jesus. Therefore, the two "like" poles are not attracted to each other. In other words, it's hard to be attracted to Jesus if you think you are Jesus. It's hard to be attracted to his holiness if you think you are holy within yourself. I'm drawn to Jesus because I am as opposite from Jesus as you can get.

This passage challenges us, and actually helps us in our preaching to the outsider, by showing us the *narrow perspective of the ecclesiastical culture*. It's helpful for us to know what we are up against when we decide to include the outsider in our preaching and our ministries. The Pharisees and scribes embody the insular perspective of the ecclesiastical culture which is not always open to preaching and ministry that draws the outsider. This culture is not always excited about the "whosoever will".

As the sinners and publicans are being drawn to the preaching of Jesus, the Pharisees and

Chapter Four

Scribes murmur, saying, "This man…" These church folks don't directly confront Jesus, they murmur. They don't complain about the fact that Jesus is preaching to sinners; the complaint is that Jesus welcomes them and eats with them. The Pharisees cannot handle the intimacy that Jesus is sharing with sinners. They say in verse 2 that Jesus welcomes them and shares time at the table with them. "Welcomes them" literally means "provides access to himself." He gives them access to who he is. He gives them access to his grace and love. Jesus' preaching and presence does not just tolerate sinners, it welcomes them. It's one thing to tolerate someone; it's another thing to welcome someone to the point of providing them access to the core of your being. Human living is not just about tolerating, it's about welcoming!

To eat with sinners and publicans is to have table fellowship with them. To have table fellowship with them is to consider them as equals. To have table fellowship is to risk contamination. The Pharisees could not imagine having dinner with unclean people because they would be risking contamination, but Jesus risks contamination to sit at the table. There's much in us which could contaminate him, but he sits at the table with us. There are some things about you and I which are toxic, but he exposes himself to our toxins and sits at the table with us in order to transform our lives. In the incarnation, Jesus risked contamination. The scandal of Christmas is that Jesus risked contamination. Jesus risks contamination because he is more confident that we will catch what he has rather than he catches what we have. Evangelistic preaching takes that risk and sits at the table with the outsider, confident that the people will catch what the gospel is infected with.

The Pharisees and Scribes criticize Jesus because of their theology. They feel so strongly about it that they insult the Savior. Included in Rabbinic teaching was this saying: "Let no man associate with wicked, not even to bring him to the law." This teaching held that religious folks were not to commune with non-religious folks not even with the purpose of bringing them into covenantal relationship with God. These religious leaders felt like their discriminatory practices were divinely sanctioned. Thus, the Pharisees and Scribes have an ignorance which is rooted in religion. This is the church culture that sometimes rebels against "outsider" preaching and ministry. Any church culture that is suspicious of drawing the outsider begins to be "cultish." At the heart of the world "culture" is the word "cult."

Jesus does not line up with their worldview, so they seek to "cancel" him. The Pharisees and scribes represent the so-called "cancel culture" which is intolerant of anything that does not synchronize with the popular worldview. In our own times, the "cancel culture" is open to free speech and free activity until the free speech offends it. The Pharisees could not handle what Jesus represented, so they insulted him. What they say is intended to be criticism, but it's actually a compliment because it confirms what Jesus said about his own purpose. Jesus already said that he did not come for the well, but he came for the sick. Their criticism is actually a confirmation, and therefore a compliment.

The ecclesiastical culture is not always open to preaching and ministry to the outsider. Magnetic preaching takes into account the feelings of some church culture, and then preaches to the outsider anyway. Church culture must understand that if we don't tailor some of our preaching and messaging to the outsider, the church will slowly die. During the height of the pandemic, I was lamenting the changes the church was having to go through. I wanted to embrace things as I had known them. I was having one of those days. I pulled into the parking lot of the church, and I looked up. Perched on the roof of the church were five large buzzards. Buzzards congregate where something is dying. God spoke to me and said if you don't change the course of some of your preaching and ministry, the church will experience a slow death. Where there is no evangelistic slant in preaching; where there is no leaning toward the outsider, the buzzards will start circling.

In these few verses of Luke, there is a challenge to model the magnetic preaching of Jesus; there is a charge to become aware of the narrow perspective of ecclesiastical culture, and there is the challenge to embrace *the heart of God in regard to lostness*. Jesus picks up on their murmuring. They are not bold enough to come right at Jesus, so they murmur. Jesus picks up on the murmuring and ends up responding.

Chapter Four

He does not respond by direct assault. He "sneaks" them. He sneaks them with a parable. The parable actually reveals the heart of God. A parable is a sonogram of God's heart. If we want to know what God's heart is like, look at a parable. The key to committing to preaching for the outsider is to be connected to the heart of God. The heart of God is revealed in this parable.

After hearing their complaint, Jesus speaks this parable. It is actually one parable, even though we refer to it as three. He tells them of the parable of the lost sheep, the parable of the lost coin, and the parable of the lost sons. In each parable there is an element of "alienation." In each case something is lost. Lostness increases with each parable. In the first one, a sheep is lost. In the second, a coin is lost. And, in the third, a son is lost. The sheep wanders into "lostness" because of its wandering nature. The coin rolls into "lostness" because of carelessness. The son walks into "lostness" because of his wastefulness. In each case there is something that is not where it is supposed to be. In each case there is something not operating according to its intended purpose. This is God's heart about the world. It is lost. Not wicked; just lost and operating outside of its purpose.

Conversely, in each parable there is an element of restoration. In the case of the sheep, the shepherd leaves the ninety-nine and goes after the one. In the case of the lost coin, the woman of the house sweeps until she finds it. In the case of the lost son, the father awaits, and at some point leaves his porch, looking and waiting, looking and waiting until his son returns. The restoration of what is lost is so important that there is both desperate seeking and anxious waiting. God loves outsiders so much that He will do whatever it takes to get them back where they are supposed to be.

And then in each parable there is a level of celebration. After finding the sheep the shepherd calls his boys and they party. After finding the coin the woman calls her girls and they party. After finding his son, the father gathers the family and they party. Evangelistic preaching and connecting with the outsider can be a joy-producer. Joy in heaven, and joy on earth! No wonder the songwriter said, "We shall come rejoicing bringing in the sheaves." The one who is brought rejoices. The one who does the bringing rejoices. The God to whom they have been brought rejoices!

Chapter Five

Under The Broom Tree: Managing the Post-Partum Blues

Elijah's reaction in 1 Kings 19 is shocking at best and humiliating at worst. We do not expect to read of the victorious prophet of Tishbe acting like this. Fear, flight, isolation, self-pity, suicide, and exhaustion are the words that now describe Elijah's life. Is this the same Elijah who faced Ahab with temerity rather than timidity? Is this the same Elijah who had unapologetically lived by faith daily at the dwindling brook; the same Elijah who encouraged the widow woman and her son through their own "pandemic"; Is this the same Elijah who had organized a competition between the deities atop Mt. Carmel?

Elijah had had enough courage to confront Ahab, enough faith to survive at the brook, enough virtue to save the widow and her son; he had enough power to defeat the prophets of Baal and had had enough patience to wait on the rain. But now, fear, flight, isolation, self-pity, suicide, and exhaustion are the words that characterize Elijah's life. The contrast is striking. Jeff Lucas has written a work about Elijah entitled *Stressed and Anointed.* The title is intriguing in itself. Normally, we do not pair "stress" with "anointing." These terms are viewed as being mutually exclusive. Lucas' title implies, however, that it is possible to be both at the same time. The reality of anointing does not safeguard you from stress, and the presence of stress does not negate the fact that you are anointed. Honesty admits that "I am not too blessed to be stressed." The difficult conundrum that exists is that I can be blessed and stressed simultaneously!

Chapter Five

Look at Elijah now. In the words of Lucas, "The ballistic missile called fear vaporized in a second the memory of all God had done for and through Elijah" (p. 91). Fear is the darkroom where negatives are developed, and Elijah now finds himself in that darkroom. The juxtaposition is disconcerting and embarrassing. The prophet plummets to a place where hope, laughter, vision, and God himself are all dead. The hero of Carmel is now a suicidal fugitive; the prophet who rebuked a diabolical dictator King is now scurrying away like a frightened rodent alarmed by a sudden flash of light. Elijah does not want to be bothered with anybody. He does not return any calls or respond to any texts. The servant, in whom he could have found support and brotherhood, is sent away. He does not return. Elijah abandons his servant at Beersheba, the southernmost tip of Yahweh's land. Elijah is right on the threshold of no longer having geographical "home-field" advantage, and he is now ready to give up. The prophet, who had brought others to life now prays that he might die. He does not only have suicidal thoughts; he actually prays that he might die. He takes his petition before the throne of mercy.

This is confusing and embarrassing. Christians do not act like this. Preachers do not have these kinds of thoughts. This is not a side of Elijah that we are used to seeing. In the words of Bishop John Gunns, "Elijah is showing himself to be a public giant and a private dwarf." Perhaps this "hidden" side of Elijah is a part of that self-awareness model called "Johari's Window". This model says that our personalities are comprised of four quadrants—one of which is known as the Hidden Self. This is the quadrant that only you are aware of and hide from others. This hidden "pane" haunts all of us and it seeps out periodically, uncontrollably when we least expect it, under the right circumstances.

Shocking or not, hidden or not, this is where Elijah ends up. The prophet ends up here because he heard about Jezebel's threat. The rumor is out that Jezebel is going to do to Elijah what Elijah had done to the prophets of Baal. Elijah hears this and he flees. This is surprising to us because Elijah had dealt with much worse than Jezebel's threat. Presently, the prophet is at a point where he is unable to handle what he could handle previously. It's not always about how severe a crisis is, sometimes it's about timing. There are

Chapter Five

some crises you can better handle on Friday than you can on Monday. Your present condition will determine how you handle a crisis.

Elijah's condition lands him under a Broom tree. A Broom tree is more like a large leafless shrub. If it's a refuge that he is looking for, Elijah picked the wrong tree. What Elijah chooses to hide under does not provide what he is looking for. What he chooses to escape under provides no real escape at all. The tree does not deliver what it advertises. The Broom tree is horticulturally symbolic of the internal desolation of Elijah's soul. Maybe that's why he chooses this tree. The Broom tree, also known as the Juniper tree, was good for very little other than becoming fuel for a fire. Psalm 120 and Job 30 speak of the Broom tree being used for charcoal. But this is where the prophet seeks refuge.

The operative questions in all of this are: How does he get to this place in life? Why does Elijah hit bottom so quickly? How do you go, preacher, from "killing the house" on Mount Carmel to having suicidal thoughts in Beersheba? How do you go so quickly from the highs of Sunday morning to the lows of Sunday evening?

Understanding this is critical for any minister of the Word so that you do not panic when this happens to you. If you have never been through this kind of emptiness just keep ministering; just continue to preach; just keep shepherding God's people; just keep investing in people's lives; just keep working with youth.

Why/how does Elijah get here? Preachers, scholars, and commentators alike have speculated about Elijah's rapid fall from the zenith of exhilaration to the nadir of desolation. Many of them conclude that it has something to do with Elijah's disappointment. Elijah comes down from Mount Carmel where he had defeated the prophets of Baal. As soon as he descends the mountain, he hears that Jezebel and Ahab are after him. The king and the queen represent Baal worship and devotion, for they had allowed it to syncretistically seep into the worship of Jehovah. Elijah, having run a great revival on top of Mount Carmel, comes down from the mountain and discovers that Baal worship is not dead. Everything occurring before his ministry is yet going on after his ministry. He operated under the ludicrous notion that his preaching was really going to make a difference. He thought that that six-week series on stewardship was actually going to increase the giving. He thought that the eight-week Bible Study series on "agape" was actually going to cause the people to get along with each other better! He actually thought that the election results that Mount Carmel produced were actually going to get rid of President Ahab and Vice President Jezebel, but he comes down from the mountain and sees that they are still in office. The result that Elijah sees is not commensurate with the work he had put into the ministry. He labored over that sermon, but it doesn't seem to be making a difference in people's lives.

In this sense, Elijah could be having what Eric Maisel calls a "meaning crisis." Maisel argues, in *The Van Gogh Blues*, that not all depression is due to a chemical imbalance, and not all depression is attributable to experiences of trauma; some depression is due simply to a search for meaning. The disparity between what the prophet Elijah believed should be happening as a result of his ministry and what was actually happening was causing him to have a crisis of meaning. Elijah was a creator, and creators deal with a search for meaning that non-creators do not have to confront. Preachers, pastors, and ministers sometimes have to navigate this type of depression because we are searching for meaning. We are looking for our work to mean something. When that meaning is absent it leads to a crisis, and we start to feel like Jeremiah who basically said to God, "You can take this job and shove it."

Perhaps this sense of disappointment and this subsequent crisis of meaning is the reason Elijah falls so hard and so quickly, but I contend that there is something else at work. The disappointment has this kind of impact on Elijah because he is dealing with "post-partum blues". We may not call it such or we may not recognize it as such, but preachers wrestle with postpartum blues.

Many new mothers experience post-partum or "baby blues" after childbirth, which commonly include mood swings, crying spells, anxiety and difficulty sleeping. Baby blues typically begin in the first two to three days after delivery, and may last for up to two weeks, and even longer in severe cases. A particular hormone is emitted throughout the body that can lead to these blues. Post-partum blues can be exacerbated by the exhaustion of having given birth. These blues can cause a sense of emptiness because in childbirth a piece of the mother has figuratively and literally gone from her. The mother has given some of herself, and therefore experiences a sense of emptiness.

Elijah was susceptible because he had given so much of himself. He preached a sermon to Ahab about there not being any rain for the next three years, that was a giving of himself. He had to go to Zarephath when the brook ran dry and help to sustain a widow and her son during the famine, that was a giving of himself. On top of Mount Carmel he had to battle with opposition, so he pours himself into prayer. He had to keep encouraging the servant to look for rain, and that was a giving of himself. In the process of parceling himself out, he begins to feel empty, which makes him vulnerable to depression. He has given birth to life for other people and now he is dealing with postpartum blues.

Real ministry, real preaching, involves the giving of self and the giving of life to other people. **Preaching at its best is the giving of self.** It is not just the exegeting of a text. It is not just the dissemination of information. It is not just the application of proper hermeneutics. It is the giving of "self". It sounds strange, it may even border on morbidity, but a piece of you dies in the process of ministry. A piece of you dies each time you preach. Paul may have had this in mind when he said to the Corinthians, "So then death worketh in us, but life in you" (2 Cor. 4:12, KJV). As Paul pours life into the Corinthians through preaching, teaching, writing, and care, he and his partners are, to some extent dying, because they give a piece of themselves each time they minister.

Death in Paul, life in the Corinthians. Preaching is about the giving of one's "self". To sweat and brood over a text is to give of yourself. To pray, think, and meditate is to give of yourself. To sit down and write out a full manuscript is to give of yourself. Sermon preparation should be a sacrificial offering of the self. It is the process of giving birth. And to stand and preach the word is an offering of self through the process of giving birth. The late Charles Booth would say that this is preaching that has "blood on it."

Chapter Five

In *Lectures to My Students*, Charles Spurgeon says that "Our work, when earnestly undertaken, lays us open to attacks in the direction of depression...." Spurgeon asks the question, "Who can bear the weight of souls without sometimes sinking?" It's impossible to carry such a heavy load without feeling like you are sinking. The task of ministry is that much more challenging because it isn't just mental work; it's heart work. Authentic preaching is a work of the heart. Giving birth to sermons week after week- month after month is heart work. The preacher is not a living specimen in preservation, but a living sacrifice.

This is the reason we feel so empty after having preached. In the same chapter in *Lectures to My Students*, Spurgeon insightfully says, "After pouring out our souls over our congregations, we feel like empty earthen pitchers which a child might break." I must admit that the Sunday evening feeling can be the strangest feeling of the week. There is an emptiness, and sometimes a loneliness that gnaws away at the soul. It's not simply because I "flunked" (preached a bad sermon) or because something went awry at church. Sometimes it's when I've had a good

Sunday. And it's not simply due to physical exaltation. It's not because I am clinically depressed. It is because of the post-partum blues. I gave birth to something, and now there is an emptiness because part of me was poured out in the moment of proclamation. Do not think it strange when you sense an emptiness after pouring out. The fact that you poured out means that a part of you is now missing. Any kind of depression intensifies after you have poured out.

Because of the post-partum blues, Elijah flees to a Broom tree. Adam and Eve lose their inherent innocence at the Tree of Knowledge. Jacob buries his family's idol gods at an Oak tree. Absalom met his fate at an Oak tree. In Zechariah's vision a man is riding amongst the Myrtle trees. Zacchaeus seeks a better seat in the Sycamore tree. Jesus curses the Fig tree, and Elijah sits under the Broom/Juniper tree. This is where Elijah seeks refuge, and on one hand, as aforementioned, this was probably the wrong tree for shelter and comfort. This was a tree, or more accurately, a leafless shrub. Under which tree do you seek refuge? You want to make sure that you are not sitting under the wrong tree. Be sure that the tree you sit under does not add to your emptiness. Under which tree do you hide? Make sure that the tree under which you hide does not add to your stress. If you're looking for something to fill the empty places, sit under the right tree, because the post-partum blues are worsened when you sit under the wrong tree. Might I suggest another tree. It's in the shape of a cross. It's located on Golgotha's hill. Under that tree you have a better chance of finding rest for your soul. Under that tree you will find a friend who sticks closer than a brother or a sister. Under that tree you will find peace that the world cannot give, and the world cannot take away.

On the other hand, maybe this is not such a bad tree for Elijah. The Broom tree was a symbol of desolation, but it was also a symbol of refreshment. The Broom bush/tree was able to survive in arid places because it had deep roots that traveled deep down into the earth and located subterranean supplies of water. That water was stored in the roots which enabled the tree to survive when it was not getting the necessary rain. Elijah was in desperate need of that kind of restoration. The preacher who is dealing with post-partum blues is in need of root level refreshment. I would imagine that a number of you have survived the postpartum blues because of what you have stored up in your roots. What you store up does not always guard against the blues, but it will sustain you during the blues.

Elijah had been up north on Mount Carmel, now he flees to Beersheba, which is as far south as he can go and sits under the Broom tree. Beersheba is just about out of God's territory. He feels like this is the place of his end. But something happens. God speaks to him at the Broom tree. This extreme case of the postpartum blues has him deciding that he is basically done with God and anything that has to do with God. Fortunately, God is not done with him. God finds him! Even when we sit under unhealthy Broom trees, God finds us. The angel taps him on the shoulder. I do not know how long Elijah was there before God showed up, but God did find him. When the postpartum blues put you under the Broom Tree, just stay there. You may not feel like praying. Just stay. God will find you. And when God finds you, God is able to fill up the empty spaces. I do not mean to glibly fling out any easy solutions to the postpartum blues, but it is true that if you sit still under the Broom tree, God will find you and God will fill you. Hence, we are justified when we sing with the songwriter:

> Like the woman at the well, I was seeking for the things that could not satisfy. And then I heard my Savior speaking- 'Draw from My well that never shall run dry.'...There are millions in this world who are craving the pleasures, earthly things afford. But none can match the wondrous treasure that I find in Jesus Christ my Lord. So, my brother/sister, [emphasis added] if the things this world gave you leaves hungers that won't pass away, my blessed Lord will come and save you, if you kneel to Him and humbly pray. **Fill my cup Lord, I lift it up Lord! Come and quench this thirsting of my soul. Bread of heaven feed me till I want no more. Fill my cup, fill it up and make me whole. ("Fill My Cup Lord")**

Chapter Six

A Refusal to go to Hell in Peace: The Role of the Prophet/Preacher in Raising the Moral Conscience of the Nation

In order for the town drunk to get to the bar he had to walk by the local church. Every day he felt like he had to sneak by the church in fear and trepidation. His hope was that when he walked by the church, the pastor would not be hanging out in the front of the church property. Many times, much to the chagrin of this brother, the pastor would be hanging out in the front of the church. The brief conversation was always the same whenever this man walked by the church.

"How are you, John?"

"I'm good, Rev..."

"John when are you going to come to church and get your life together?" John, who heard this almost every day, would give the same response, "Reverend, I'll be there this Sunday!" This went on week after week; month after month; year after year. One day, John was taking his typical route to the bar. As he approached the church, he saw the pastor standing out front. He prepared himself because he knew what was coming. This time John was a little tipsy because he had been sipping at home even before he went to the bar. The pastor said to him once again, "John please come to church and get your life together for your sake and for the sake of your family..." John, who had grown tired of hearing the same thing day after day, and because he was feeling bolder on this afternoon, said to the pastor, "Reverend, will you just let me go to hell in peace!"

One of the reasons we celebrate Martin Luther King is because he refused to allow America to "go to hell in peace." In this sense, King was one of America's rare heroes. He was not a hero in the sense of moral or strategic impeccability. Michael Eric Dyson says, "A heroic figure undeniably possesses the ability to substantially alter and influence the course of events because of her mix of personal traits, skills, talents, and visions" (*Dyson Reader*, p. 289). King's work helped to alter the downward slide of the country. America was headed to the hell of the further hardening and calcification of racism and the subsequent, inevitable violent confrontation between the races. King was that preacher who stood in front of the church and "got on the collective nerves" of this country. He wouldn't allow the nation to pass by him without him saying something.

Perhaps that is the role of the prophet/preacher. Getting on the collective nerve of the community and indeed the country is the task of the church, the preacher, and the prophet. The purpose of this Holy irritation is to help shape the moral conscience of the leaders of the nation as well as the nation itself. Dietrich Bonhoeffer did it in Germany; Bishop Desmond Tutu did it in South Africa. The prophets did it in the scriptures.

In the Hebrew Scriptures there was this strange, eccentric figure known as the Nabbi, whose job it was to help shape the moral conscience of the king and the people of Judah and Israel. Nabbi means to "bubble up". Something inside the prophet "bubbles up" to the surface as the result of divine influence. The prophet did not just "come up with sermons". The Nabbi preached under the influence. Nabbi also means to "speak up." The prophet must speak up in order to vent what has "bubbled up." The prophet has nothing to say when he/she speaks up if nothing has "bubbled up." Jeremiah, because of the pressures of ministry, decided to quit. He turned in his resignation papers, returned his ordination certificate, and decided that ministry was not for him. The preacher of old would say that Jeremiah was comfortable with that decision on Monday of that week. He maintained the comfortability on Tuesday, Wednesday, Thursday, and Friday.

Chapter Six

But "long" about Saturday he became uneasy and concluded that he had to say something because what was in him was like "fire shut up in his bones." Something had "bubbled up" therefore he needed to "speak up."

James D. Newsome points out that there were two important types of prophetic guilds in ancient Israel: cult prophets and court prophets (Newsome, p. 6). The cult prophet, which was the older of the two, operated within the confines and context of the Jerusalem Temple. This prophetic guild spoke primarily to those inside of the house of God. The cult prophet delivered oracles from God to the people. The cult prophet also served in the priestly capacity of offering sacrifices and receiving the people's petitions to God. Beyond that, the cult prophet came to have special responsibility for the poetic and musical aspects of the liturgy, and many scholars view certain of the Psalms of the Old Testament as having been composed by the cult prophets attached to the Old Testament (Newsome, p. 7). As the monarchy evolved in Israel the "court prophet guild" emerged.

The court prophet's duty was to speak to the king concerning matters of the well-being of the nation. Whereas the cult prophet ministered within the temple, the court prophet operated within the palace. The court prophet had the ear of the king. There was no such thing as sacred and secular in the life of Israel. Therefore, the court prophet operated in a sphere of politics, economics, and the military. The court prophet was a part of the cabinet of the king. The king was wise enough to have a prophet in the vicinity. In some cases, the court prophet grew too close to the king and subsequently was afraid to speak truth to power. If the king was helping to put bread on the table of the court prophet, the prophet was more likely to speak what was expedient and not what was prophetic. In the words of Dr. William Watley, "It was critical for the prophet to maintain a healing closeness to the King, but also a healthy distance from the king."

The court prophet needed to be "close" enough to speak, and far enough away to "speak." In any case, the court prophet's role was to help shape the moral conscience of the king.

As is the case with many of us, King operated as both cult prophet and court prophet. King's early work and ministry was primarily that of a cult prophet as he led the congregation of Dexter

Chapter Six

Ave. church. However, the climate jettisoned him into the arena of being a court prophet. The climate of the nation forces cult prophets to also operate as court prophets. To exclusively minister to the cult without any word for the court is like playing in the band making beautiful music as the Titanic is sinking!

Eventually King's attention turned almost exclusively to that "court." Martin King was the court prophet who was instrumental in shaping the thought and practice of President John F. Kennedy. At the heart of Steven Levingston's book, *Kennedy and King*, is the contention that it took a prophet to teach a president! Kennedy was the wealthy Irish Catholic president; King was the Southern Baptist preacher. The two had a natural rapport. It was King, more than any other figure, who led Kennedy to finally make a moral commitment to civil rights. It may be that King's greatest contribution to the Civil Rights movement was not the protests, marches, and sermons in themselves; it was what these activities did- they called the president into accountability. Martin King got on Kennedy's nerves!

The best example may be the Birmingham case. What happened in Birmingham, Alabama may be the best example of how the prophet pricks and shapes the conscience of a nation. Birmingham, which was also called Bombingham, because of the terrorist activity of racist groups, became the epicenter of the fight against segregation in 1962 and 1963. Jim Crowism was present and pervasive in Birmingham. Blacks were not allowed in certain eating and shopping establishments. "Whites Only" signs were everywhere. Wyatt Tee Walker put it best when he said, "We knew that as Birmingham went, so would go the South." The problem with this is that it created an intractable sense of inferiority in those who were excluded, particularly in the souls of children. Contrariwise, it created a sense of inflated superiority in those who did the excluding. Martin King, Fred Shuttlesworth and others sought to change this by drawing attention to what was happening in Birmingham, but King's primary objective was to seize the undivided attention of President Kennedy so that he would act decisively by enacting federal laws. King engaged various strategies to speak to the nation and

Chapter Six

particularly to the White House. He participated in demonstrations himself. His associates were surprised to see him come out of his room at the Gaston Hotel one afternoon in the spring of 1963 in his blue jeans rather than his typical dark suit. It was his plan to go to jail that day. It was not by accident that King ended up in the Birmingham jail. There was some intention behind it. During that same spring, Dr. King encouraged and helped to organize youth participation in the marches and demonstrations. Consequently, jails were filled with young people. This was meant to weigh on the conscience of the president and others around the world.

One of the most potent forms of applying pressure to Kennedy was through King's words. King did this by preaching sermons in mass meetings. His preaching was in the context of the "cult", but he spoke toward the court. Most of King's sermons in Birmingham accentuated the need for action "now." Kennedy's administration embodied and promulgated a philosophy of gradualism. King challenged this in his preaching. Martin King also used the power of words in interviews that he knew would reach the ears of the White House.

In a 1963 interview with *Look Magazine*, King complained that the president had brushed off the bombing of black churches, the shooting of blacks, and the denial of voting rights. King blasted the president for failing to give the same passion to civil rights that he gave to other domestic issues such as steel prices (Stevenson, p. 308). The effective use of words reached its zenith in "Letter from Birmingham Jail" which Martin King wrote on toilet paper. One of his most poignant "sermons" was written on toilet paper from a cold jail cell! Included in this letter were these words that King knew would reach the president:

> ...we must come to see that human progress never rolls in on wheels of inevitability. It comes through the tireless efforts and persistent work of dedicated individuals who are willing to be co-workers with God, and without this hard work, time itself becomes an ally of the forces of social stagnation. We must use time creatively, forever realizing that the time is always ripe to do right. Now is the time to make real the promise of democracy and transform our pending national elegy

into a creative psalm of brotherhood and sisterhood. Now is the time to lift our national policy from the quicksand of racial injustice to the solid rock of human dignity. ("The Other America")

These words bubbled up in the soul of the prophet and he had to "speak up." This message was intended to reach President Kennedy, and that is exactly what happened. Eventually the president learned from the prophet. Kennedy sent federal troops to Alabama. His aides began drafting legislation that would give the government the power to speed up the integration of public facilities. Most dramatically, in 1963, Kennedy delivered an address in front of a live national audience in which he answered a call to his own conscience by raising the moral issue associated with racism and segregation. Steven Levingston says in his address that, "Martin Luther King Jr. was present in the president's voice, in his words and in his conscience. Intentionally or not, Kennedy had absorbed the language and themes of King's "Letter from Birmingham Jail", a copy of which had been delivered to the White House." King was not allowing the country to go to hell in peace. He raised the moral conscience of the president primarily through the proclamation of the Word. Martin King was not the last court prophet to function in this capacity. There is another prophet who performed the same task and filled the same role long before Martin King did. His name is Nathan. He was David's court prophet. Nathan was to David what King was to Kennedy and what we are to the powers that be. Nathan offers us a paradigm for prophetic proclamation that assists us in raising the moral conscience of the church, the community, the nation, and our elected offcials. Nathan shows up when David was considering building the temple. Nathan also shows up during the debate over who would be king after David, Solomon or Adonijah. Nathan shows up after David's fling with Bathsheba and the subsequent murder of her husband.

After David's actions he seems to be able to rest comfortably. Uriah, Bathsheba's husband is now out of the way. Bathsheba has been vouchsafed to David and they're able to live out their "Little

Chapter Six

House on the Prairie" existence. However, it's not too long before it becomes a "Nightmare on Elm Street", and the peace is disturbed. Chapter 11 of 2 Samuel closes by saying, "...the thing that David had done displeased the Lord." Chapter 12 opens with, "Then the Lord sent Nathan to David." Because God is displeased, God sends a prophet. God would not allow injustice and immorality on the part of the king to go unchecked. The king needed to be held accountable. The king is not above moral law. The king was not above the law of the land. Therefore, God sends a court prophet to David in order to raise David's moral conscience. Nathan does this by means of the proclaimed word. There are several ways to elevate moral conscience, but our most accessible and impactful way may be through the proclamation of the Word of God, whether that be through preaching, writing, or whatever forms are at our disposal. Nathan's proclaimed word is a word that is imaginative. Nathan does not come at David with the facts of the situation. Instead, he tells the story about a rich man who prepared a feast for his guest. Instead of getting a lamb from his own flock, he steals the one lamb his poor neighbor owns. After hearing this parable, David became angry at this rich man and thus indicted himself. The parable sneaks up on the king and catches him off guard. He believes it is about someone else.

C.H. Dodd said that a "parable is a metaphor or simile drawn from nature or common life, arresting the hearer by its vividness or strangeness, and leaving the mind in suffcient doubt about its precise application to tease it into active thought" (as cited in Sweet, p. 107). The story, the image arrests the heart. The Swedish filmmaker, Ingmar Bergman, once said that facts go straight to the head, but stories go to the heart. Jesus used parables to the end of arresting the hearer and teasing the mind into active thought. Prophetic preaching that raises the conscience does not always have to be so direct. It is not always characterized by direct address. There are times when direct address is necessary. There are other times when skilled, imaginative images may be used to speak truth to power. The preacher of the Gospel pays attention to the effective use of words, images, stories, and metaphors. This is a way of raising the moral conscience of the church, the community, and the nation in a creatively

Chapter Six

disturbing way. One of the factors that made Martin King different was his imaginative use of language. Martin King constantly used images, metaphors, and parabolic language in his sermons and speeches. Keith Miller contends, "King's unmatched words galvanized blacks and changed the minds of moderate and uncommitted whites...King did so by translating the message of the imaginative black folk pulpit into the idiom of a Harry Emerson Fosdick" (as cited in Miller, p. 11).

King did not always speak directly about the demise of his enemies and the enemy of justice, namely evil. Instead, he preached the image of the Egyptians washing up on the seashore. The image arrests the hearer, and before the hearers know it, they are teased into active thought and transformative contemplation. The word of Nathan to David is also a word that is *honest*. After hearing the parable, David gets angry and declares that the rich man who stole the lamb from the poor man deserves to die. The pronouncement of judgment on another is much easier than owning one's own offense. Immediately, Nathan, the court prophet speaks some of the most disconcerting words in all the Bible: "You are the man." What inescapable words these are! The word of the prophet only indicts David after David had indicted himself. "YOU are the man." Nathan could have been beaten, imprisoned, or even killed for his words, but he spoke them nevertheless. David is commended for receiving the words. The words of the prophet mean little to a King who is so drunk with hubris that he cannot see himself has having done anything wrong. Gardner Taylor's prophetic preaching was unique in that it was simply honest about the human condition. In the end, prophetic preaching is just honesty. It's not always angry, loud denunciation. Sometimes it is simply quiet, passionate honesty. It is honesty about the environment. It is honesty about distribution of wealth. It is honesty about family relationships. It is honesty about corruption. In order for the preacher-prophet to be honest in preaching, in order to raise the moral conscience of the nation and the king, the prophet needs to be somewhat maladjusted. Adjustment implies acceptance to the status quo. Prophets were strange. John the Baptist was not "quite right." Harry Emerson Fosdick laments the fact that the well-adjusted life settles down into contentment with the status quo (as cited in Miller, p. 107). Fosdick continues, "...the deepest obligation of a Christian...is to be maladjusted to the status quo" (as cited in Miller, p. 107). In order to help readjust society, the prophet has to be maladjusted to the current arrangement. The Nathans of the world cannot adjust to behind-the-scenes political conniving. The Nathans cannot be afraid to declare, "You are the man." Nathan's proclamation, which was intended to raise the moral conscience of the king was imaginative, honest, and it was *hopeful*. Prophetic preaching without the element of hope is nothing more than the venting of pent-up frustration. Included in Nathan's last words to David was this affirmation: "The Lord has put away your sin, you shall not die." Even in the darkness of David's context there was yet a light of hope. Undergirding the proclamation of the cult and court prophet is hope.

One of the miracles of history and of the kingdom of God is how slave preachers in the midst of horrific circumstances, were able to transmit hope through their preaching. Eugene Genovese remarks that without slave preachers' affirmation of hope amid immense hardship, slaves might not have endured it all (Miller, p. 18). Slave religion promised salvation in both this world and next. The eschatological was imported over into the existential and it provided a foundation of hope. To preach is to import the eschatological into the existential; the not yet into the now.

Contemporary ministers of the gospel of Jesus Christ probably should not preach unless there is kernel of hope at the core of the Kerygma. The raising of the moral conscience includes a hopeful vision of the not yet. That vision empowers us in the now. Augustine says, "Hope has two beautiful daughters: anger and courage. Anger at the way things are and courage to ensure they do not stay the way they are." This hope was at the center of Nathan's word; it was the throbbing heart of King's message, and it must be at the foundation of our own proclamations.

There was a song that I used to hear the old folks sing at the Refuge Baptist Church and the Mt.

Chapter Six

Period Baptist Church in Columbus, Ohio. I did not quite understand it then, because I did not recognize the deep-seated hope that refused to let my fore parents live in hell in peace. They sang:

> When your way seems dark and drear, you don't have to worry cause God is near. If in your heart there is no song, just keep the faith and keep holding on. Turn your face down, fast and pray. Jesus will always make a way. There's a Bright side [emphasis added] somewhere ("There's a Bright Side Somewhere")

Chapter Seven

Keep Your Turban On: The Challenge and Necessity of Preaching through Adversity

EZEKIEL 24:15-18

Life, and even the Lord, have some strange ways of preparing you for a sermon, lecture, or presentation. Life will test you to determine whether you really believe what you are preparing to say. God will add some authenticity to your preached word by allowing you to experience existentially what you are preparing to say homiletically. God makes sure that what you are about to say, you believe. The Lord really wants Hosea the prophet to be able to preach the truth that God is married to the backslider. He doesn't want the prophet to merely speak from what he has gleaned and gathered from a commentary. Therefore, he commands Hosea to marry Gomer. When Hosea stands before the people, he is able to exude the pain and pathos of having been betrayed the same way Jehovah had been betrayed by the people of God. God has a way of making sure you ain't just talking!

Ever since I've been thinking about this whole idea of preaching through adversity a few months ago, it seems as though life has thrown and the Lord has allowed me to experience adversity on different levels. You have to be careful about what you are preparing to say or preach, because the Lord will test and shape you in that particular area.

Most recently our congregation experienced, what felt like, the sudden death of a member

Chapter Seven

who has had a positive influence over many people. She was a leader in our church whose spirit of love encouraged a number of souls. This lady loved a number of our youth as though they were her own. One youth, in particular, happened to be my own daughter, who referred to this lady as her "New Jersey grandma." So, I had to watch the tears stream down my daughter's face the moment she heard of the passing. In addition, this sister was close to me. She was one of those folks whose countenance made preaching easier. The Sunday after her death and right before the "Home-going" service, there was a spirit of heaviness in the worship atmosphere. I could tell that many people were sad and not in the mood for "praise and worship." I knew that because I was one of them. Yet and still, I had to stand and preach. I had to be the prophet who spoke on behalf of God, and I had to be the priest who spoke on behalf of the people. The day of the funeral service was difficult as well. We celebrated her life, but I was mourning along with everyone else. Right before I got up to preach the eulogy, the soloist sang one of those moving songs, and subsequently, a number of people began to visibly grieve. I felt what they felt, yet I had to pray for composure. Why? Because I had to get up as the prophet and speak on behalf of God to the people and speak on behalf of the people to God.

I had to preach through the adversity. This is not just my challenge. This is your challenge as preacher, minister, and teacher. If you haven't had to preach through some personal or church adversity yet, it is certain to come. Life brings different seasons, and you can't quit just because you're going through a tough one.

This is Ezekiel's challenge in Ezekiel 12:21. Take note of the prophet's adversity. "The Word of the Lord came to me..." There's nothing the prophet can do or say until the word of the Lord comes. The Word is not organically born in the preacher, it comes to the preacher from a source outside of the preacher. Before the word of the Lord comes to the people, it comes to the prophet.

The prophet is accustomed to the Word of the Lord "coming" to him. However, he didn't expect this Word. This is the last thing Ezekiel wanted to hear from God. "...with one blow I am about to take away from you the delight of your eyes" (Ezekiel 24:16, NIV). This is a tragedy of which God is the source. The devil has nothing to do with this. This word comes from the Lord.

The pain of the loss is felt as Ezekiel's wife is referred to as the "delight" of his eyes. There was a deep, intimate relationship between the prophet and his spouse. Jehovah doesn't even identify Ezekiel's wife. He simply says, "the delight of your eyes." It's clear who that is. With "one blow" she is to be taken from him. She may have had a disease which had fatal consequences; we don't know, but what we do know is Ezekiel and his wife are going to be severed by the "dark divorce of death."

The prophet is not exempt from adversity. Ezekiel's prophetic pedigree does not exclude him from the company of sufferers. The fact that Ezekiel is preaching two and three services per Sunday does not exempt him from trouble. The fact that people view him as their leader and their priest does not lift him above the possibility of pain.

I hope it's not news to you that preachers are not exempt from adversity. It was the late Dr. A. Louis Patterson of Mt. Corinth church of Houston, Texas who said, "God only had one Son who could hang a sign outside that says, No Sin Here. But God has had no sons or daughters who could hang a sign outside that says, No Hurt Here." Your "anointing" does not elevate you above adversity; sometimes it makes you a target for adversity and attack. Your Masters of Divinity degree does not mean you have graduated from the school of hard-knocks!

Charles Spurgeon, who was called the "prince of preachers" by his own son, knew much adversity. Author John Piper, in an address on preaching through adversity at a pastor's conference in 1995, holds Spurgeon up as one who preached through adversity. The English preacher of decades ago experienced a life of trouble. As he preached at Royal Surrey Gardens to about 10,000 people, a fire broke out and 7 people were killed. He was held responsible for that. After the birth of his twins, because of some cervical condition, Spurgeon's wife was rendered unable to have any more children. Spurgeon himself suffered with severe gout, rheumatism, and Bright's disease. As if that weren't enough, he dealt with criticism both inside and outside of his church. Joseph Parker, a fellow preacher, who should have been a support for Spurgeon, criticized him as being "absolutely destitute of intellectual benevolence." Spurgeon had deacons in his church who constantly second-guessed his decisions.

Like everyone else, preachers and prophets know both internal and external adversity. Like everyone else, we have loved ones who die. Like everyone else, we have seasons of financial strain. Like everyone else we have marital conflicts which don't always end positively. We have children who go astray. On top of that we have to endure church stress and tension. It's not unusual to have to deal with power struggles with church leaders. There are times when certain people, in the words of the Apostle Paul, "seek to do you much harm." And then internally you struggle with your own inadequacies and insecurities. You are haunted daily by the ghosts of what you could have done differently. You live with a mentally draining and sometimes deranging sense of second-guessing. Perhaps the ministry has not brought you all you thought it would. You live with the torture of having not accomplished what you set out to accomplish.

Ezekiel's season of adversity is predicted. His wife is going to be taken from him suddenly. The word of the Lord gets strange at this next point.

After we note the prophet's adversity, a turn is made with the mention of the prophet's sobriety. Ezekiel is informed tragedy is coming his way. And then he is told that he is not permitted to mourn like everyone else. The Lord says, "Yet do not lament or weep or shed any tears." Mourning in ancient Israel was a demonstrative ritual. For a number of days, there would be the tearing of clothes; removing of shoes and turbans; shaving the head; covering the face, and even rolling in the dust. It was meant to be a communal, demonstrative ritual.

Ezekiel is commanded to not participate in any of this. There is something not fair in this. There is something unnatural in this command. God seems to be expecting too much of the prophet. He just lost his wife. Ezekiel is indeed human, and he will be crushed by this death. Yet God says he can't grieve like everyone else. This does not seem right.

Notice, Ezekiel is not told that he can't grieve at all. V. 17 says "groan quietly." God does give the prophet space to grieve. Even a prophet needs space to be human and vent her/his frustrations. Not being able to grieve or to vent would lead to mental instability. The prophet needs space

Chapter Seven

to be human, and God gives him that exact opportunity. There are times when even the prophet needs to "pull over" and be human. A number of clergy are living with internal agony and anguish now because of the inability or unwillingness to "let it out" in a safe space. God gives the prophet some room for this.

However, he is told that he has to subject his personal grief to his public duty. The prophet has an extra responsibility. He is to maintain a level of sobriety. He can't do it like everyone else. One of the penalties of his prominent position is that he has to forfeit his right to the public demonstration of his emotions. In adversity, outside of adversity, you are still the prophet. Mature leadership knows it can't always display personal feelings. It's not about being fake, it's about being responsible to your calling. The preacher, because of his/her concern with human needs and identification with God's purpose, has to pay a heavy price. You are called again and again to surrender your private life to the requirements of your public responsibility. In the case of this text, the one who must bear a nation in his heart may not indulge his individual griefs as others do; his task remains, and it demands all his energies.

In the middle of this command from the Lord, Ezekiel is instructed to keep his turban on. Many times, the priest and prophet wore a turban indicating it was time to work. To remove the turban meant a relinquishing of or at least a rest from duty. The Lord says to Ezekiel, no matter how you feel, keep your turban on. The prophet is told that he can grieve, but that he needs to keep his turban on. The challenge of Christian ministry is being able to deal with what you deal with personally and at the same time "keep your turban on." The challenge of Christian ministry is being able to minister in the midst of your own misery. The demands of the kingdom are such that we can't afford to take our turbans off. No matter how angry we get with members, we can't take our turbans off and become something other than what we've been called to be. What amazed me the most about President Obama's administration, was how he was able to keep his "presidential turban" on even when he was under constant attack from detractors who clearly had issues with his pigmentation rather than his policy.

This text accentuates the adversity of the prophet, the sobriety of the prophet, and then it

Chapter Seven

shines a light on the responsibility of the prophet. Verse 18 always amazes me: "So I spoke to the people in the morning, and in the evening my wife died. The next morning, I did as I had been commanded." I'm sure it's not as simple as the text reads, but the next morning Ezekiel kept his turban on and ministered to the people. What do I do the next morning? What is my response the morning after "life happens"? Because, what happens at night has the power to ruin my morning. What did he do the next morning? We know nothing about how Ezekiel felt; we only know what he did. The text is not interested in how he felt. It is interested, however, in what he did. Keeping your turban on is not about how you feel; it's about what you do.

Ezekiel preached through his adversity. It is a part of our duty to preach/minister through adversity. In his book the *Under the Unpredictable Plant*, Eugene Peterson notes that years ago in Eastern Europe, pulpits were in the shape of an upright whale. Peterson says that in order to take his place as a preacher, the pastor or priest had to enter the interior of the pulpit at the base, climb a ladder through the belly, and then come into the open mouth and deliver the sermon.

Peterson remarks that this is accurate architecture, because every true gospel vocation is a resurrection vocation that arrives after a passage through the belly of the fish. Many of us, just like the runaway prophet Jonah, have to pass through something which should have destroyed us, on our way to the pulpit. None of us come to the pulpit "clean." We have passed through the belly of something. Some of us are thrust into the pulpit by the force of whatever gripped us all week. Even though God spoke to it in enough time for us to make it to the place of ministry, we still may wear the stench of what we've been through. Can you imagine how Ezekiel smelled? All of us come to the pulpit by way of the belly of the fish.

John Piper puts it another way. In his article, "How Charles Spurgeon Learned to Preach through a Broken Heart", he says, "...the heart is the instrument of our vocation." Piper goes on to tell us that according to Spurgeon, "Ours is more than mental work- it is heart work, the labor of the inmost soul." As a result, Piper concludes that when our heart is breaking, we must labor with a broken instrument. It's easier said than done though. How do we minister with a broken heart? How do we preach through adversity? In *Preaching Through a Storm*, H. Beecher Hicks Jr. admits that a storm provides an unnatural, alien, even hostile environment in which preaching with power becomes nearly impossible. "In the evening my wife died...In the morning I did what I was commanded..." How do we do that? There is no easy answer. There are no three points and a poem response to that question. But here are some things to think about which may help us to keep our turbans on.

In order to keep our turbans on we have to *refresh ourselves through rest and prayer*. I was almost ashamed to include this idea because it is so basic. Rest and prayer, really? I know you already know this. But if the prophets are going to be able to preach through adversity, they need to take care of themselves and stay in touch with the Almighty God. The inner person is strengthened through communion with God. The prophet is neither invincible nor indispensable, therefore we have to know when it is time to go to the back of the boat and sleep on a pillow even when the waters are choppy. Learn how to rest even in rugged waters.

In order to keep our turbans on, preachers must *recognize that to preach in adversity is the nature of the gospel anyway.* The gospel is good news. That good news is good news in a context of darkness. Preaching great and glorious truth in an atmosphere which is not great or glorious is difficult. But therein is the nature of the gospel revealed. The gospel was made for the darkness of personal and congregational adversity. In creation the words "Let there be..." were spoken into an atmosphere of darkness and chaos. It was dark out in the rolling, lonely hills of Palestine when the shepherds received the news, "For unto you is born this day in the City of David a Savior..." The darkness of what you are going through does not contradict ministry or preaching, it provides the backdrop for the good news. To preach even when you are experiencing the dark night of the soul symbolizes the nature of the gospel. According to Peter, between crucifixion and resurrection, Jesus descended into hell and preached to the spirits. That is the nature of the gospel. Jesus takes resurrection to hell. Every time we preach in the midst of adversity, we are taking resurrection to hell. The gospel is birthed from darkness and born for darkness. Keep your turbans on.

Chapter Seven

We're able to keep our turbans on when we *rebel against despair and bitterness*. It is easy to fall into bitterness and despair when you are dealing with personal adversity. But the preacher has to literally rebel against it so that you don't take the bitterness to the pulpit. Sometimes you have to wage an outright rebellion against your own emotions in order to avoid bitterness. When we take bitterness to the pulpit, we will start fighting those people who have caused us trouble, from the pulpit. We will write an entire sermon on the backs of a few folks who have been giving us trouble and ignore the needs of the masses who simply need to hear a word from heaven. The late Dr. Manuel Scott Sr. once said that every Sunday when you go out to preach you have a combination of lions roaring and lambs crying. The lions represent your opposition; the lambs are those whose hungry souls need to be fed. He says that we will ignore the cry of the lambs in order to aim at the roar of the lions.

In keeping our turbans on we have to *refrain from making our experience normative*. The temptation when preaching through adversity is to use the pulpit as a therapy session. I have to be careful not to make my experience the source of my sermon instead of the Word of God. If I do that, I will put everyone in the congregation where I am. Just because I'm in pain doesn't mean everyone in the congregation is. If I write several sermons on pain just because that's where I am, that may not be where everyone else is. I might be broke, but not everyone in my congregation is. I might be prospering, but not everyone in my congregation is. I can't preach as though my experience is normative for everybody.

In order to keep my turban on, I have to r*ely on my adversity to feed my preaching.* I just stated that adversity should not control my preaching such that every sermon is about what I'm going through. However, I cannot divorce my preaching from my existential reality. I don't have to, and I shouldn't. What I am going through feeds my preaching because it enables me to connect with the reality of the human plight.

When the Lord told Ezekiel about what he was going to experience, and how he should respond, he was actually preparing him for a message he wanted him to preach to the people. The people, because of imminent invasion and exile, were going to have the delight of their eyes taken from them. And the Lord desired for them to continue to represent him to the world even though they would go through this tough season. Ezekiel's personal experience would be the energy that brought genuine passion to what he needed to say to the people. His mess would put some "blood on his preaching". Dr. Charles Booth says effective preaching has some blood on it. Bloodless preaching is preaching done by a preacher who has not experienced some level of adversity and therefore can't really connect with the people. Don't go looking for adversity but do know that adversity puts some blood on our preaching. Our Christ is not bloodless; therefore our preaching can't be bloodless. Our cross is not bloodless, as a result, our preaching can't be bloodless. Our salvation is not bloodless; hence our preaching can't be bloodless.

It was difficult but the prophet was commanded to keep his turban on. The adversity gets thick sometimes, but keep your turban on. The sorrow is gut-wrenching at times, but keep your turban on. The opposition is fierce at times but, keep your turban on!

Chapter Eight

Beyond Mechanics: Accessing Power for Preaching

LUKE 4:14

The skies were blue. The sun was shining. The breeze was relatively calm. The seagulls were effortlessly flying above hovering the waters as skilled hunters waiting to descend upon the surface of the sea in search of small fish. I was sitting in a beach chair looking out on the Gulf of Mexico when I noticed something strange. Two people were on something called a Hobie Cat. A Hobie Cat is a small sailing catamaran manufactured by the Hobie Cat company. It resembles a small, narrow sail boat contraption that has a large sail towering up into the air. The Hobie Cat that these two people were on was beautiful. It was a bright blue, about the same color of the sky. It was sleek and sophisticated looking. The boat appeared to be brand new. The two people occupying the boat seemed to be skilled at what they were doing. I could tell that they weren't novices. They had some kind of official gear on as though as though they were professionals in sailing. The problem, however, was that they were having a hard time getting their boat to glide across the water. With their best effort, the boat was not going anywhere. All the mechanics were in place, but the boat was not going anywhere. Professionals were operating the boat, but it wasn't going anywhere.

The next day I sat in the same spot. The skies were blue. The sun was shining. The seagulls were again hovering above. But the wind was fierce. Ironically, I saw those same two people on the

Chapter Eight

same Beautiful Hobie Cat. This time they did not seem to be exerting much effort, and the boat sailed rapidly across the waters. It was the same boat; it was the same waters; it was the same two men on the boat. What was the difference? It was the wind.

In the preaching enterprise all the mechanics can be in place, but if there is no wind, the sermon is not going anywhere. If there is no wind the sermon may be admired but it will not be impactful. If there is no wind, the assessment may be, he/she "killed that house", but no lives will be changed. The wind is power. The wind is the Spirit of God that fills the sails of the sermon and enables it to move from where it is to where it should be.

All the mechanics can be in place. The exegetical work has been done. The sermon has been written with precision. The preacher can be adorned in clergy garb or a fine suit or dress. However, wind is required for movement. Most "preacher talk" is about mechanics. Most books written on preaching focus on mechanics. Most conferences on preaching accentuate and analyze mechanics. I understand this because we can control mechanics. And there is a critical need to converse about mechanics. But there's probably not enough attention paid to the power that is required in order for preaching to be transformative.

It goes without saying that mechanics and assiduous labor are critical for effective preaching. Dependence on the wind is no excuse for laziness in preparation. The mechanics are the setting of the sail. The wind fills the sails so the boat can move. But if no sail is set, the wind will be wasted. The boat only moves because of the combination of a prepared boat and steady winds. It's up to the preacher to set the sails; it's up to the Spirit to fill the sails with power. Effective preaching requires mechanics and power. Gardner Taylor said that "Sermons are born of a mysterious romance between preparation and inspiration." James Earl Massey put it another way:

> The way of a preacher with a sermon is marked out for him/her by two basic influences: nature and grace. The influence of nature is seen in the preacher's intellect,

temperament, gifts, and training. The influence of grace is seen in how these natural factors are enlisted and enhanced by the touch of God.

Mechanics, technique, and preparation are all necessary for transformative preaching. The proclaimer of the Word has to avoid the temptation of not preparing in anticipation that the Spirit is going to get the job done. Awaiting the "move of God" is not reason to neglect work. Charles Haddon Spurgeon tells the story of the Bishop of Lichfield who came to town and lectured to preachers on the importance of study and the diligent investigation of the Word. One of the preachers stood up after the Bishop's presentation and said, "When I'm in the pulpit I do not know what I'm going to talk about, I just depend on the Spirit. I go to the pulpit, preach my sermon, and think nothing of it." At this the Bishop replied: "you are quite right to think nothing of your preaching Sir, because I've spoken to some of your members, and they share your opinion!"

Mechanics, style, and preparation require a great deal of attention. However, a concomitant power has to be accessed in order for preaching to be transformative. The aim of preaching is to impart and to impact. We impart a person who will impact people. Preaching does not simply dispense information; but preaching imparts a person. Massey contends that a part of preaching has to do with the God-given ability to project an awareness of God in connection with the presentation of Biblical truth. A presence is conveyed through the preaching of the Word. We don't just talk about Jesus through our preaching Jesus actually shows up. In essence Jesus told Martha, after she articulated her belief in the eventual resurrection that what she was looking for she was looking at. I agree with Phillips Brooks, "It is good to be a Herschel who describes the sun; but it is better to be a Prometheus who brings the sun's fire to the earth." The hope and prayer of every preacher is to bring the sun's fire to earth! The purpose of this fire, indeed the purpose of this presence which comes through truth is to change lives. We preach to change lives. Like anyone I appreciate comments from people who say that they "enjoyed the sermon". It's a "false humility" that says it does not appreciate "pats on the back." However, that is not the purpose of preaching. The ultimate aim of preaching cannot be to get more engagements. The

Chapter Eight

ultimate aim of preaching cannot be "get my name out there." The ultimate aim of preaching is to change lives and thereby glorify the One who has called us.

It is impossible to affect this kind of change without power. One of the loneliest feelings for the preacher is to stand and not "feel" the presence of the Lord as you preach. When there is the feeling of the absence of presence and power the preacher "sweats the sweat" of panic long before he/she sweats the sweat of effort. Have you ever sweated the sweat of panic? The sweat of panic commences when you feel as though you are up there by yourself. Even if the folks are not saying amen, you at least want to feel God's presence. This sense of the of mysterious power is what we used to call "unction". This charismatic concept is scary to some of us as preachers. We associate it with anti-intellectualism. We associate it with some kind of possession. Frank Bartleman, an itinerant holiness preacher of the early twentieth century, preached during the Azusa Street revival. He says that in that setting "God flooded my soul with power." This is what Bartleman called "unction." It's that part of preaching that you cannot control, but you just have to be open to. James Forbes believed that much of the weakness of contemporary preaching is attributable to a Holy Spirit shyness among Christian preachers.

Transformational preaching requires power! The Christian preacher is the successor of the Hebrew prophet not the Greek orator. The Greek orator, although influential, solely depended on logos, pathos, and ethos; logos being speech, pathos being passion; ethos being the integrity of speaker. The Hebrew prophet had all of that plus the anointing of the Spirit. Jeremiah might not have had the eloquence of a Demosthenes, but he did have more power! Therefore, as preachers we find our roots in the Hebrew prophet not the Greek orator. Jehaziel had very little to say to Jehoshaphat and the people until the power of the Spirit fell upon him. Isaiah had very little to say to Jerusalem until his lips were touched by the live coals from off the altar. "How gloriously a preacher speaks when his/her lips are blistered with live coals from the altar!" Peter had very little to say to the folks who thought the people of God were drunk in the upper room until Pentecost fire had fallen on him.

Power is required because the because the preacher is the mouthpiece of the Spirit. The

Chapter Eight

Spirit becomes the speech teacher of the preacher, and the preacher, the mouthpiece of the Spirit. This is what Rudolf Bohren calls Theonomic Reciprocity. There is a reciprocal relationship between preacher and Spirit. Power is required because the sermons we create are always less than the texts we use. At best, we hover around the outskirts of a text because of our human limitations. The power of the Spirit makes up for our sermonic deficiencies. Power is required because, in our preaching, we engage the principalities and powers that sit in high places and oppress the people.

If power is required to impart and impact, from whence does such power come? This is a strange question because power is not something you can harness. Power for preaching cannot be manipulated, but it can be accessed. The power is not in the volume of the voice. The power is not in the intensity of the histrionics. From whence does this power come. How can it be accessed? It's a strange phenomenon because you cannot explain why some preaching moments are filled with power and some are not. However, maybe we can make it a practice of setting our sails so that the wind can fill them.

How is power accessed? The witness of our Christ may help us to answer this question. Luke 4:14a says, "Jesus returned to Galilee in the power of the Spirit." As Jesus went to the Wilderness he was "full of the Spirit." When he returns from the wilderness, he is in the power of the Spirit. Jesus returns "in" what he left "full of." As he went to the wilderness the Spirit was in him. When he returns from the wilderness he is in the Spirit. In the power of the Spirit means that his identity has been subsumed into the person of the Spirit. To be in love is to be consumed by what you are in. Jesus is about to commence ministry in the power of the Spirit. In the everyday living of life, we want to be full of the Spirit; in the preaching of the Gospel, we want to be in the power of the Spirit.

How is power accessed? Why was Jesus able to return in the Power of the Spirit? There is no "one, two, three" formula for this. However, there are some simple truths that may facilitate the filling of our sails with the wind.

Jesus returned in power and commenced ministry in power because he took the RISK OF SOLITUDE. I say "risk" because solicitude is risky.

Chapter Eight

You see and hear things about you that may be disconcerting. Jesus was led into the wilderness by the Spirit. He was led into isolation for the sake of solitude. Mark and Matthew imply that Jesus was led into the wilderness to be tempted. Luke implies that Jesus was simply led into the wilderness for the sake of solitude and happened to be tempted while he was there. Jesus was by himself. Solitude is required in order to access power for preaching. After studying Spurgeon's sermons, Helmut Thielicke concluded that Spurgeon had the gift of "charismatic hearing". By that he meant that Spurgeon first lingered in the presence of God to hear God speak before moving forth to say anything on God's behalf. It's difficult to speak on God's behalf in public if God has not spoken to you in private. To access power the preacher must be faithful in the discipline of solitude. "Discipline" because solitude does not find you, you have to find it. The preacher who is scurrying about trying to keep up with every member and meet every need may miss out on the power that comes forth from solitude.

Jesus returned in power and commenced his ministry in power because of the INTENSITY OF

STRUGGLE. Jesus did not create this struggle, it just happened because of where he was. He was alone. The devil tempted Jesus. The struggle is born of the internal wrestling match with Satan. It wasn't as though Satan was some external force sitting next to Jesus mouthing seductive temptations. Satan was speaking to the mind of Jesus as Jesus was attempting to figure out how he would win the world. The temptations are in the form of alternatives to doing it God's way. The devil was more interested in perversion than in prevention. The enemy knew that he could not prevent the ministry of our Christ, but he thought he could pervert it by presenting alternatives. Jesus knew that the cross was the only way to do it. The enemy presented the alternatives of bread, power, and miracles. The enemy knows that most of us are too strong to get us with preventing, but he also knows that we may not be strong enough to resist perverting.

The bottom-line is that Jesus endures a season of struggle. That season of struggle gives birth to power. No one wants a season of struggle. We try to avoid seasons of struggle. But seasons of struggle give birth to power. Struggle puts some blood on your preaching. Charles Booth once

Chapter Eight

said that preaching must have blood on it in order to be powerful. In his sermon on "I Know that My Redeemer Liveth", Dr. Gardner Taylor rhetorically asks the preachers, "Do you want great power to move among men's heartstrings? You cannot have that without great struggle and sorrow. God can fill only that place that has been emptied of the joys of life." Don't go looking for struggle; but do know that great power is born of struggle.

Jesus returned in power and commenced his ministry in power because of the PRACTICE OF SELF-DENIAL. I really do not like this one so much. I tried not to include this truth. Jesus said "no" to real temptations. Turning stones to bread in order to attract a following was a real temptation. If it was not real, it never would have entered the mind of the Messiah. Temptation requires both desirability and accessibility. Jesus desired to turn stones to bread, and the stones were right in front of him. But, he was able to say no. The struggle for Jesus in the wilderness was self-denial versus self-indulgence. It is difficult to experience power if I never say no. Consistent indulgence short-circuits my power.

Jesus returned in power and commenced his ministry in power because of his CONFIDENCE IN SCRIPTURE. As you well know, to each temptation Jesus responds with "it is written." The only response that could handle real temptation was "It is written." Logic was not adequate. Temptation laughs at logic. Intellect could not do it. Temptation mocks intellect. The Word of God was the only adequate response to temptation.

Jesus responds like this because he actually believes in scripture. He believes in it beyond the public declaration of it. The temptation of the preacher is to only have confidence in the Word at the preached moment. The question is: Do I believe in private what I declare in public? Belief in scripture in private leads to power in public proclamation.

Jesus returns in the power of the Spirit for the sake of ministry. The preaching enterprise is too difficult to attempt to do it without the power of the Spirit. The wind enables us to do "backdraft preaching." Mark Buchanan coined this phrase. Backdraft refers to the phenomenon when a fire subsides because it's burned up all the oxygen in the room, and then suddenly oxygen-laden

Chapter Eight

air rushes in (perhaps because of an open door) and sparks an explosion. Fresh wind meets a dying fire! Many times my preaching was a dying fire, but the fresh wind of the Spirit sparks an explosion. When I want to quit, fresh wind meets a dying fire! At that point I concur with Jeremiah...

Chapter Nine

From Fans to Followers: A Textual Consideration of the Aim of Pulpit Preaching

JOHN 1:35-42

It was during the spring of 1984 when I was scheduled to preach what may have been my first revival at the Shiloh Baptist Church of Newark, Ohio, where Dr. Charles Noble served and still serves as pastor. I was finishing up my freshman year at Denison University. During that academic year I had been exposed to the likes of James Cone, Tillich, Bultmann, and so forth. I was filled with the arrogant, pomposity of a college freshman who knew it all. On that first night of the revival, I just knew I was ready to "slay the house." I had on my freshly cleaned, ninety-nine dollar, black Gino Cappelli suit. The waves in my hair were laying just right. My black Stacy Adams shoes had been immaculately polished. I had sprayed on some Stetson cologne. I knew I was looking good. And I knew that my sermon was ready. I sat in the pulpit anxiously awaiting the time that I could stand before these people so that they could observe my homiletical skills. The pastor introduced me; the choir sang an "A" selection, and I stood up. As I stood up in my pride, something happened that shall live with forever. I looked down at the wooden pulpit podium, and on it was etched these words "Sir, we would see Jesus."

I had come there with that aim. I really wanted this congregation to see me. Those words shattered my hubris. Those words haunt me to this day. The pastor intentionally placed those words there, so that whomever stood to preach

Chapter Nine

would be reminded of what the aim of their preaching is. It might seem like a small matter, but it is essential that preachers be in touch with the aim of preaching. Why are we doing this? Why are you writing these sermons? Why are you mulling over these passages of scripture? Why are you reading these commentaries? Why are you doing this? Why are you doing all of these revivals and conferences? Why are you on the road so much? Why are you preaching these multiple services? Why are you rushing off from one location to another on Sundays? Why are we sacrificing vital relationships, health, and energy to do this thing called preaching? You sweat! You're hoarse all the time. You get irritable because you're tired. Why? Is it ego gratification? Is it the money? Is it simply the fulfillment of an obligation to a "calling"? Is it to get my name out there?

I have to be aware of the "aim" of preaching. If I am to do this thing with some level of integrity, I must be able to answer this question of: Why am I doing what I am doing? If I am not consciously and intentionally cognizant of my aim, I will be like Winnie the Pooh. One day Winnie the Pooh was walking in a circle around a tree, making tracks in the snow. Tigger asked, him, "What are you looking for?" Winnie said, "I don't know." Tigger went on, "Well, if you don't know what you are looking for, how will you know when you find it?" Winnie the Pooh responded, "If I don't know what I am looking for, I surely will not know when I find it." My preaching will simply be making tracks in the snow if I don't know what the aim of my exercise is. If we don't know our purpose and aim, we will be guilty of what Dr. Cleophus LaRue called mounting "pulpits without purpose." In a lecture with the very same title, LaRue contends that when preachers get so caught up in preaching the new and the now, they forget about the crux of our assignment, and that is to preach the "unsearchable riches of Christ", we will indeed fall victim to preaching from pulpits without purpose.

If we are not in touch with the aim of preaching, we will see "sermonizing" as an ends in itself. There are some people who want to hear preaching because they are "sermon tasters." They go from church to church; from revival to revival; from conference to conference, looking for "good preaching." There is no intention on making any changes in either the loving of the

Chapter Nine

Lord or the living of life. They just like good preaching. Preaching is almost artwork to be admired. Because that is the case, preachers are tempted to craft sermons to please the ears of "sermon tasters", instead of crafting sermons to change the hearts of people. Sermonizing on exciting passages of scriptures takes the place of the declaration of the kerygma when preaching becomes an ends in itself. The question that the preacher has to ask as she/he writes sermons and mounts pulpits is: What is the aim of this sermon? What is this sermon intended to do? What is to be produced from this moment? Sometimes what I thought was the aim ends up being shifted based on the needs of the hearers and the intervention of the Holy Spirit. In other words, the sermon may do something other than what I thought it would do in the life of a particular hearer based on where they are. The Holy Spirit is in better touch with the needs of the people than I am. So, from the time that the Word leaves my mouth until the time it reaches the ear of the hearer something miraculous happens. The Spirit repackages what I have said in order to meet the need of the one who sits there. There is another agent between the speaking preacher and the hearing congregant, and that is the interceding Spirit. The Spirit of

God, at a rate faster than the speed of sound, shapes what is said to speak to the soul of that brother or sister who is on the verge of giving up. The Spirit of God is actively engaged at the moment of preparation. But he is just as involved at the moment of proclamation, by giving you fresh insight that you may not have even gotten in the study; and by transforming the word once it leaves your mouth. I cannot manipulate the ultimate purpose that a particular message may have in the life of the congregation. However, I can at least have some sense of what the intended purpose is.

H. Grady Davis, in his work, *The Design of Preaching*, advises preachers to pay attention to the function of preaching before we become too preoccupied with the form of preaching. For Davis, function, that is to say, the "why" of preaching, precedes the form, that is to say, the "how" of preaching. Function and form are closely related. The function of the sermon determines the form. The aim of proclamation is what determines the nature of the structure, style, and the delivery. When it was Jesus' aim to educate his disciples in the principles of the kingdom, he used a very deliberate, conversational form as he sat with them on the hillside and declared the beatitudes. The function was the foundation for the form. When it was the aim of Jesus to denounce the hypocritical practices of the Scribes and Pharisees, Jesus employed an "in-your-face", direct style which left no room for ambiguity. H. Grady Davis believes that the function of preaching has to be established a-priori in order to shape the form.

John the Baptist demonstrates what I contend is one of the primary functions of preaching: "to turn fans of the ministry (and for that matter the minister) into followers of the Messiah." In v. 35 we read of two of John's disciples standing there with John. In v. 37 we read of those same two disciples choosing to follow Jesus. From John to Jesus! What happened in between? In between this adjustment in allegiance there is some preaching. They hear what John has to say, and they end up following Jesus. I wonder, does that happen after I preach? I wonder, is that the result of my preaching? John, having seen Jesus in the vicinity, points to Jesus and says, "Behold, the Lamb of God." Therein is a primary function of preaching!

In chapter one John has some fans. They are attached to him. His ministry had been so effective that the people gravitated toward him. His preaching was powerful, direct, and engaging, so the people surrounded him from everywhere. And I can appreciate it because there is nothing wrong with people appreciating the ministry of their leader. There is nothing wrong with folks who have been blessed by a certain ministry expressing their gratitude for the life-changing gospel which a particular preacher preaches. It is biblical and logical for members to look out for the leader, and to be sure that he or she is taken care of. Beyond that, it makes sense to be excited about the one through whom God is working in your midst. There is nothing at all wrong with pouring into, providing for, praying for, and protecting the servant of God.

But John understands that it is not healthy to have people too attached to who he is. There is an understanding of *temporality* in John's ministry. It is subtle. And I hope I am not reading too much into it. But I believe in "gospel in the grammar." Don't ever ignore the gospel which is hidden in the grammar. V. 35 literally reads, "The next day John stood with two of his disciples." A portion of v. 36 reads, "Jesus was passing by…" It is telling that "stood" is in the perfect tense, whereas "passing by is in the present tense." The perfect tense in the Greek language is that tense which denotes a completed action. It's done. It had its time. It had its season. John "stood." Jesus is "passing." Whatever John was doing, it was done. Whatever Jesus is doing, he was doing it. John's ministry had a fixed time limit to it. He was only going to be on the scene for a while. And John was conscious of that. The action of God through Jesus of Nazareth was a present reality that was moving. The action of God in Christ is always a present action.

Every preacher must know that your ministry is always a "perfect tense ministry." The day will come when it will be a completed action. It is only the move of God through Christ which is eternally in the present tense. You and I will be off the scene when the move of God is continuing. We needn't become deluded into thinking that our significance will always be in the present tense. I could be off the scene tomorrow. I could pass from time to eternity next week. The church would have a service. They would mourn. They would take my remains to the cemetery. Come back to the fellowship hall. Eat chicken, potato salad, green beans, and drink Kool-Aid. My picture would be placed alongside the other former pastors, and they would go on with the work of the church. No matter how exhilarating and fulfilling your ministry is, understand that it is a perfect tense ministry. The action will be completed. Success may give us the illusion that we are indispensable and invincible. Death shatters that illusion. It was the Communist leader Vladimir Lenin who said that the church in Russia would die with the grandmothers. Well, the church in Russia has continued to thrive, but Lenin is "good and dead." Even though they tried to preserve his body, he is still "good and dead." He had a perfect tense administration.

This is why it is dangerous for us to build ministries around ourselves. We will be off the scene. And then what? As soon as we are gone, the ministry crumbles. Honestly speaking, it might be ego-gratifying to have a ministry which is centered around the preacher. But that does very little for the future of the kingdom of God. John's ministry was characterized by temporality.

There is an understanding of *invisibility in* John's ministry. He says, "behold, the Lamb of

Chapter Nine

God." "Behold" means to fix your gaze upon. "Behold" means to give this your undivided attention. John now wants to be invisible. It sounds strange saying it, but John's main competition is Jesus. I once heard Dr. William Curtis say in a presentation he was giving some years ago, that the primary competition of the preacher who seeks attention is Jesus. Our main competition is not the pastor down the street. It is Jesus. The more I preach the Christ, the more the allegiance of the people will be attached to him instead of me. The stage is only large enough for one: either me or the Lord. Both of us cannot fit on the stage of the people's souls.

John understood that the stage was not large enough for him and Jesus, thus he had a ministry of invisibility. Listen to the words of John 1:6-9:

> There was a man sent from God, whose name was John. The same came for a witness, to bear witness of the Light, that all people through him might believe. He was not that Light but was sent to bear witness of that Light. That was the true Light, which lighteth everyone that comes into the world.

Listen to John's own words: "I must decrease that he might increase."; "There is one who comes after me who is preferred before me, because he was before me."; "There is one here whose shoes I am not worthy to untie."; "I indeed baptized you with water, but there is one here who will baptize you in the Holy Ghost." John is aware of what H. Grady Davis points out concerning the importance of all parties involved in the preaching scenario. Davis says that in order of importance, the Sender is first, that's the Lord; the Substance is second, that's the gospel; the Saints are third, and that's the congregation; and the Servant is fourth, that's the preacher.

John is not a sight to be seen in the wilderness, he is a voice to be heard in the wilderness. The aim of the preacher is to be as invisible as possible. Obviously, you have to be visible to preach. Preaching, according to Philip Brooks is, "truth through personality." So, then our personalities can't help but to be present. Our personalities, with some level of creativity, need to be present. But I never, as a gospel preacher, want more personality to be present than truth. Personality of my dress, decorum, and disposition can't be more pronounced than the truth. Nothing wrong

Chapter Nine

with looking good when you stand up; however, as I hear my father in life and in ministry saying to us as young preachers you don't want what you have on to be louder than you are. There are very few preachers who simply stand "flat-footed" who declare truth. The whole body of the preacher is now involved in the moment. And that's alright as long as our antics, histrionics, gestures, and body movements don't become the substance of our presentation. Sometimes the truth of what we're saying gets lost in the artistry and performance of our presentations. John has a ministry of invisibility.

There is an understanding of *intentionality* in John's ministry. His aim in preaching is to intentionally point to Jesus Christ. "Behold, the Lamb of God..." Preaching is pointing. Behind Karl Barth's writing space –the workspace where he wrote Church Dogmatics –there is a reproduction of a painting by Mathias Grunewald called *The Crucifixion*. The painting shows Jesus hanging on the cross. To the right of Jesus on the cross is John the Baptist who is holding an open Bible with his left hand, and a finger pointing toward the cross with his right hand. The figure of Jesus is large in portrait, and John's body is relatively small, to symbolize John decreasing and Jesus increasing. John's finger with which he points to Jesus is disproportionately long. It is exaggerated to show that this was John's primary ministry. And it is our ministry. Sunday after Sunday we hold the open Bible with one hand and point to the cross with the other hand. The aim of preaching is to point to the crucified/resurrected Christ.

John points to Jesus in his preaching because he has some fans whom he wants to become followers. A number of people who come to our churches are fans of the minister, the ministry, and movement, but are not yet followers of Christ. There is a difference between fans and followers. Fans only want to hear you preach and will not tolerate anyone else preaching. You can't tell fans that you won't be there, or else they will not come. Fans are fair weather. They will be with you as long as things are going well. But they will abandon ship if they sense the ship is sinking. Fans are excited when everyone is speaking well of you. But they might leave you when everyone is not speaking well of you. My dad might say that fans have dynamite testimonies, but firecracker

Chapter Nine

faith. And that lack of faith shows itself when the going gets tough. I live in an area which has some tough sports fans. In the New Jersey/New York area the fans are hard on their teams. If the Yankees are winning, the people worship them like gods. If the Yankees are losing, the fans are booing them and looking for other teams to root for. But the followers are with Yankees through thick and thin. They are there when everyone else is turning their backs on the team. As a preacher you want followers of Christ and not fans of the preacher. Fans of the preacher seem to be with you at first. And they will make you feel like you are somebody. But, let it get too hot! They will be nowhere to be found. Followers of Christ, on the other hand will be there for the ministry, even if the ministry is in a difficult season. Fans will give as long as they are happy. Followers will be faithful to giving and tithing even if they are mad at you for a minute. Jesus had plenty of fans after he fed the five thousand. As soon as he preached one sermon on commitment in Jn. 6, they all turned back from following him. Jesus turned to the twelve he had left and said, "Will you also go away?" Peter said, "To whom shall we go?" That is a sign of a follower and not a fan. Fans will be with you during your triumphal entry into Jerusalem but will be in hiding during your Friday crucifixion. And it is tempting to be satisfied with having fans, because fans pop-up automatically, without much intention. It does not take much work to build a congregation of fans. Followers have to be developed over time. Followers have to be discipled. But it is worth the time it takes to develop followers. Followers will work. Followers will dream big dreams. Followers will be there to help bring the vision to fruition.

John preaches in this first chapter with the intent of transforming his fans into Jesus' followers. Twice he says, "Behold the Lamb of God." He says it in v. 29. He says it again in v. 35. It was a continual message. The only way for him to turn his fans into followers was consistent preaching. The one thing which stands between fans becoming followers is the faithful, weekly proclamation of the Word of God. This is what it takes for us as well. It takes some preaching with some depth to gradually transform people. It takes the consistent exposition of the Word in the context of worship to make this transformation. In this period, I don't know how many times John had to repeat this line. It is recorded twice in this chapter, which indicates he had to say it more than once. There are some themes that the preacher has to "hit" continually in order for the congregation to "hear" it. That kind of preaching may not always have "snap, crackle and pop", but it will lead to growth.

John's short sermon has depth. Preaching that changes fans into followers is preaching that is consistent; it is also preaching that has some depth. In our attempt to reach "seekers", "Baby Boomers", "Generation Xers" and so on, we reduce preaching and worship to its barest bones. I understand the need to be contextual in order to reach people. Paul did say, "I become all things to all people so that by all means I might save some." But we have to be careful stripping preaching, liturgy, and worship of all its majesty, mystery, and doctrinal substance. John's message was fundamentally doctrinal: "Behold the Lamb of God, which takes away the sin of the world." It may take one kind of preaching and worship to reach people; but it may take another kind to grow the people who have been reached. At some point some level of doctrine and majesty need to be worked into our preaching and worship. This is only if you want to transform fans into followers. Some years ago, I remember my sister was doing all she could to get my nephew, who was a toddler at that point, to eat some baby food that had a little substance to it. He would not want to eat anything like the Gerber's peas or the chicken and turkey baby food. If it wasn't sweet, he would not eat it. To make sure he ate something, she would give him the applesauce and the pears. But I noticed that gradually she started mixing the sweet "stuff" with the substantive "stuff", and the boy ate it and grew. Good preaching may mean mixing some of the "substantive stuff" with the "sweet stuff"! It's alright for us to preach on themes of grace, love, sin, justice, and sanctification! Fans won't become followers if all we tell them every week is this your season of prosperity!" "This is the week of your breakthrough!"

Finally, there is a sense of *reality* in John's preaching and ministry. The reality is that there are some things that Jesus can do that John can't do. This is why he points beyond himself.

Chapter Nine

John is the sign that points to the substance. The preacher is to the salvation moment what the golden arches are to McDonald's. If you are hungry and you are traveling down the highway. It is the symbol and sign of the golden arches which will get your attention and cause you to get off the highway at a particular exit. When you get off the exit you don't go to the arches to eat. If you went to the arches and just stopped there, the arches would tell you, "I can't feed you. Go inside. That's where the food is. You can look at me if you want to. But you will not get full by staring at me." John understands that Jesus can do for the people what he cannot do, that is why he says in v. 29 "Behold the Lamb of God, which takes away the sin of the world." John can't take away the sin of the world. John can point out the sin, but he can't take it away. That verb "take away" (airo) can mean both "to transfer" and "to remove." This brings to mind the image of the Scapegoat in Leviticus. On the Day of Atonement, the priest gets a goat, takes his hands and puts them on the head of the goat and confesses the sins of the people. Everything that is confessed is transferred to the goat. All of the sin is taken from the people and put on the scapegoat.

They wouldn't just transfer all of their sins onto the goat and then leave him there. They would also remove the goat from the city limits. The sin was "toxic", so they had to get the goat out of town. The goat was led to the wilderness and then the goat would either fall over the ledge or they would push it over the ledge. The death of the goat meant the death of whatever was transferred to the goat. John points to Jesus because that is what Jesus does for us. He became sin for us who knew no sin. And then he took all of that to the cross and died for us. John says, "I can't do that." We preach Jesus because he can do what we can't do! Jesus can make lives brand new. I can't do that! Jesus can send demons packing. I can't do that in my own strength.

All four gospels basically declare, "Behold the Lamb of God!" This means that we're entering a whole new phase of history. The fundamental question of the Old Testament is articulated by young Isaac right before his father is about to sacrifice him: "Where is the Lamb?" John the Baptist looks at Isaac and declares, "Behold the Lamb of God!" One day, when it's all over, the

Chapter Nine

question will not be, "Where is the Lamb?" The statement will not be, "Behold the Lamb!" But the exclamation will be, "Worthy is the Lamb!" We needn't wait to declare that. We can declare it right now: Worthy is the Lamb. Worthy is the one who took our sins. Worthy is the one who was raised early Sunday morning!

Chapter Ten

Are We Bored With Jesus?

Rediscovering and Reclaiming the Nature and Necessity of Christocentric Preaching

The existential philosophers say that in order to live life with integrity people have to answer two fundamental questions: "Who am I?" and "Why am I here?" The likes of Jean-Paul Sartre and Albert Camus contend that existence precedes essence; that is to say that we are born and then we must discover our purpose. If we are to live with some sense of meaning these questions must be answered. If we are to wage a war on the "absurd" these questions must be answered. If we don't answer these questions, says Sartre, "life will be like hell with no exit."

Those questions are critical to living with integrity, but there are three other questions which are critical to preaching with integrity. Preaching is what we do. Preaching is essential to the very life of the church. Preaching shapes the beliefs of congregants. As the church preaches, the church believes. Therefore, it would behoove us to seek to preach with integrity. If we are going to preach with integrity, there are at least three questions which must be considered: 1) What are we preaching? 2) Who are we as preachers? 3) Why are we preaching? There is no doubt that we cannot ignore the "how" of preaching; but the "how", that is "style and delivery", are not as crucial as the "what", the "who", and the "why". I understand that the "how" of preaching is often most apparent and visible. The "how" sticks out to us. It is accessible. It is conspicuous. Style and delivery jump out at us. As a young, impressionable preacher, attending the National Baptist Congresses and Conventions,

Chapter Ten

it was the style and delivery of preachers like Manuel Scott Sr., Caesar Clark, E.V. Hill, and A. Louis Patterson that immediately seized my attention. There was much substance to their sermons, but as a younger preacher it was their style which spoke to me first. I would go back to my hotel room and practice some of their gestures as I looked at myself in the mirror. I was trying to figure out how I was going to combine the inimitable gestures and voice inflection of Manuel Scott with the lyrical melody of Clark with the humor and boldness of E.V. Hill, with the humble sophistication and structured presentation of Patterson. It was the "how" that grabbed me. But as visible as the "how" is, it is not as essential to the issue of integrity as the "what", the "who", and the "why." The "how" of preaching is not to be underestimated, for effective style and delivery make the preaching moment complete. However, the "how" is not the priority of our purpose.

Each of these aspects of preaching is essential, but the one that I want to focus on is the "what" of preaching. What are we preaching? I understand that we preach something different just about every Sunday. But my question is what is at the core of our preaching. What does our common message "boil down to"? If someone asked you, "What do you preach?" What would you say? The question is not, "What are you preaching this Sunday?" The question is, "What do you preach?" We preach our series. We do special occasion preaching. We preach in conferences which have particular themes. We preach to cast vision in our churches. But underneath all that we preach, what is it that we are saying? My contention is that **underneath all of our preaching there has to be a theological and homiletical substratum from which all of our preaching emanates**. There must be a kerygmatic core to our preaching. I noticed that in the campaign speeches of former President Barack Obama, as there is with most presidential candidates, there was a thematic core at the center of most of what he said. The title of one of his books is, *The Audacity of Hope*. That sense of "hope and "yes we can" is what was at the center of most of what he said. If he was talking about health care, hope was at the center of it. If he was discussing education, hope was in the middle of it. If we don't have a kerygmatic core or a theological substratum, we will be guilty of "onion preaching." If you peel back all the layers of the skin of an onion, there will be nothing left, because an onion is nothing more than the sum total of its peelings. If we don't have a core to our preaching, you'll be able to peel back all of the skins or our points, our moves, our illustrations, and our cute anecdotes, and there will be nothing. We don't want to be guilty of "onion preaching."

The Challenge of Christocentric Preaching

It might sound too simplistic; it might sound too obvious, but it is nevertheless true that at the heart of Christian preaching there must be Jesus Christ. As "Sunday Schoolish" as it sounds, I have to reaffirm the truth that the theological substratum from which all of our other preaching must emanate is the Christ event. At the core of our weekly sermons, there has to be a Christocentric focus. Don't take this for granted, because sometimes we preach everything but Jesus. It was Joel Gregory who made a very troubling statement to a group of preachers during a conference: "Preachers seem to be bored with Jesus." That troubles me. That keeps me up at night. I wonder if that is true. Are we bored with Jesus? Have we graduated from Jesus? Did we leave Jesus back in Vacation Bible School? Has all of our "deep revelation" pushed Jesus out from the center of our preaching? Has our thirst for something new to say moved us beyond the manger, the cross, and the empty tomb? I wonder if we have become too sophisticated for, "Yes, Jesus loves me, for the Bible tells me so"?

Are we bored with Jesus? I hope that is not the case because I agree with Cleophus LaRue who poignantly remarked in his lecture *Pulpits Without Purpose* that: "If we forget to preach Jesus Christ and Him crucified, we run the risk of preaching from pulpits without purpose even though our churches may be on the cutting edge of change and bubbling over with worldly success. I hope this is not the case because I agree with Gardner Taylor who said that "All of our preaching is suburban until it comes down onto the central place, which is Jesus. Here is the centerpiece of our preaching..." The preaching of Taylor is often held up as a model for preachers in any generation. The one thing you can say

Chapter Ten

about his preaching is that it was/is saturated with Christ and the Christ event. For Taylor, Jesus the Christ is the "glue" which holds our preaching together. Recently I was taking a walk through the park, and I saw a man who must have been a professional dog-walker (they have these now!). He must have been walking about six dogs at one time. He had about three leashes in one hand, two in the other hand, and maybe one wrapped around his arm. It sounds like chaos, but it was very orderly. I watched it, and I said to myself, "That man is to those dogs what Jesus is to our sermons." Those dogs found their centeredness in the man to whom they were attached. That man provided those dogs with direction, and their attachment to him kept those dogs from running off and doing someone harm. When our sermons are not tied to the Christ event, they have no direction, and they might run off and bite someone and do them harm. Christ is our centeredness in preaching. Are we bored with Jesus?

What are we preaching? What's at the bottom of our sermons? It was Paul who said to the Corinthians, "But we preach Christ crucified..." In the very next chapter he says, "For I am determined not to know anything among you save Jesus Christ, and him crucified." What are we determined to "know" among our people? I am afraid that we might be tempted to "know" everything but Christ and him crucified. What are we determined to "know" among our people? We preach everything but him. There is a temptation in our preaching to make "applications" of the gospel the core of the gospel. Prosperity, healing, faith, deliverance, self-actualization, and compassion and social responsibility might be "applications" or consequences of the gospel, but they cannot become the core of the gospel. And I know that they have become the core of my preaching when that's all I preach! If material prosperity seeps into all of my preaching, then I know that that has become the theological substratum from which all of my preaching emanates. And whenever I do that, I might become guilty of idolatry. Whenever any theme, other than Christ and Him crucified, becomes my constant focus, I make that theme an absolute and I fail to see the other side. If deliverance and breakthrough are the only things I preach, then those thematic emphases become idolatrous absolutes. And it will give my people the impression that God is only active when God is delivering you from the fire. An application of the gospel might be that God is a healer. But if I make that an absolute, then my people will think something is wrong with them or with God if they are not being healed. It is possible for some of our so-called preaching themes to become idol gods! When I preach Jesus and him crucified, it helps the listener understand that God is not just a God who blesses with "deliverance", sometimes he blesses with "endurance." Our idol gods may be some of the homiletic themes that replaced the core of the gospel message.

The Logic of Christocentric Preaching

Why? Why should Christ be the one theme that permeates our sermons consistently? I would like to suggest some reasons why. First of all, *The Christ-event can be the lens through which we view other passages of scripture and preaching themes.* When Paul said, "But we preach Christ crucified" and "For I determined to know nothing among you, save Jesus Christ and him crucified", the apostle is not saying that Jesus Christ and him crucified is the only thing that he preached. There were many evangelistic, pastoral, prophetic, and relational themes that Paul dealt with. And he was contextual as he spoke to a myriad of issues. When Paul says, "I determined to know nothing among you except Jesus Christ, and Him crucified", he was definitely suggesting that the person and passion of Christ were at the heart of his message. But he may be also suggesting that the Christ event is the lens through which he preached other themes. To preach Christ "does not necessarily mean to seek to discover where Christ is mentioned in every text, but to disclose where every text stands in relation to Christ" (*Christ-Centered Preaching*, Brian Chapell). Preaching Christ does not merely mean mentioning the name of Jesus Christ in a sermon. It is not the artificial super-imposition of Jesus on every Old Testament text. Preaching Christ does not simply mean attaching to the end of the sermon the familiar lines: They hung him high and stretched wide, and he died, til' the sun refused to shine. He died, til' the stars flip-flopped in their silvery sockets. And they buried him in a borrowed (borrowed because he wouldn't need it long) tomb. He stayed there Friday night. He stayed there all day Saturday, and even Saturday night. But early Sunday morning he got up with all power in his hands." Somebody ought to say that every time they

Chapter Ten

get a chance, but preaching Christ means more than lyrically concluding with those references.

Christ can be the hermeneutical lens through which we view texts we preach and topics we declare. The lens you look through determines what you see when you look. What you say, and how you say what you say, sounds different because of what you saw when you looked. We say what we've seen. And what we've seen looks different depending on the lens through which we look. Even preaching on the "judgment" or "wrath of God" looks different through the lens of Christ and his cross. There was a particular pastor in a church who preached about hell every Sunday. Every Sunday he preached: "Y'all goin' to hell." Some of the church leaders pulled him aside and said, "Reverend, you might want to preach about something else sometimes." The pastor insisted on preaching the same thing: "Y'all goin' to hell." The church tired of that, and ended up getting rid of that pastor. One day that former pastor came back to visit that church. He sat in the back and just observed. The new pastor preached, and throughout his sermon he kept saying, "Y'all goin' to hell. But the former pastor noticed that the members were shouting and clapping. People joined when the invitation was extended. The former pastor was confused, so afterwards he gathered some of those same deacons around him and said, "This preacher is saying the same thing I was saying". The deacons said "Yes, he is saying the same thing. But Reverend when you said, "Y'all goin' to hell", you sounded like you wanted us to go!"

How we say what we say is different when we say it from the vantage point of the cross. Christ-centered preaching enables us to stand on Calvary's hill and view everything else we want to see and then say. From the vantage point of Calvary, the expulsion from endemic paradise in Genesis 3 looks different. From the vantage point of Calvary, the consistent dysfunctions of God's people in the Old Testament look different. From the vantage point of Calvary, it's hard not to preach liberation for oppressed peoples. Are we bored with Jesus?

Another reason that Christ should be at the center of our preaching is because *it makes our speech distinctive*. To simply preach moralistically; to simply preach ethical platitudes; to simply preach human self-

Chapter Ten

actualization; to simply call people to doing justice, without any reference to the carpenter from Nazareth makes our speech nothing more than motivational speaking. Gospel preaching is not gospel preaching without Christ being at the center of it. We have to be careful when our preaching, writing, lecturing, "gospel" singing, and our ministries, period, fit in too well to our culture. That may mean that we have sanitized them of the Savior. Because anything that is too "Christ-centered" is probably not going to make it on the New York Times best-seller list. Anything that is too "Christ-centered" is probably not going to be warmly embraced by media outlets. If I can take my sermons, preach them in a non-Christian setting, and no one is offended, that may mean that my sermons have been "Savior-sanitized." The Sanhedrin court tried to sanitize the preaching of Peter and John. They said to them, "We really don't mind y'all preaching. We don't mind you 'slaying the house.' We don't mind y'all quoting the great philosophers. But please don't heal or preach in the name of Jesus!"

I do not mean to imply that we need to be dogmatic, insensitive, or unnecessarily narrow-minded. But there ought to be something distinctive about our speech. Great oratory is not what makes our speech distinctive; the Greek orators, who believed in the Pantheon of Greek Gods, could probably beat all of us in oratorical skills. Exhortation in ethical responsibility is not what makes our speech distinctive, for the teachings of Islam encourage great moral responsibility. The call to justice and social activism is not what makes our speech distinctive, some of the Eastern religions endorse compassion and justice. Reverence for the Almighty is not what makes our speech distinctive. One of the seminal convictions of Judaism is a holy fear and respect for Yahweh. What makes our speech distinctive is Jesus Christ our Lord. And so, I wonder, "Are we bored with Jesus?"

Why preach Christ and him Crucified? We preach Christ and him crucified because *it's a theme that is always relevant*. Jesus does not need much help being relevant. Manuel Scott Sr. said that there is a "relentless relevance" about Jesus. Christ is always contemporary. Themes come and go. Sometimes we get caught up in preaching what is trendy. But if you want something that is always in vogue, say something about him. "The gospel we preach," in the words of Gardner Taylor, "is a Gospel that does not belong to any particular age, but it does belong to every age." On one occasion a group of Jews, in the gospel of John, told Jesus that they did not need him because they had Abraham. Jesus said to them, "Before Abraham was, I am." "Was" applies to Abraham, but "is" applies to Jesus. He is the eternal "is", about whom there is never a "was." "Was" applies to Moses, but "is" applies to Jesus. "Was" applies to Muhammad, but "is" applies to Jesus. There is nothing wrong with being creative when it comes to preaching this gospel. There are some creative minds out there that are declaring this gospel in some innovative, fresh ways. Praise God for that! But just know that our Lord doesn't need much help being relevant. Jesus doesn't always need hip-hop references along-side of him to be relevant. Are we bored with Jesus?

We are admonished to preach Christ and him crucified because *Jesus is able to meet the fundamental needs of humanity*. That is a salient theme of the New Testament in which I yet believe. We preach Jesus because we believe he's able to meet the needs of broken and bruised humanity. It was Howard Thurman who wrote in *Jesus and the Disinherited*, that "The religion of Jesus is for those whose backs are against the wall." Jesus meets the fundamental need of freedom and liberation. Abraham Maslow's primary contribution to psychology is what's known as Maslow's Hierarchy of Human Need. He says that there are seven needs that are intrinsic to human personality. He says our most basic need is for the physiological (food etc.). He lists the rest in chronological order of the most fundamental: safety; love and belonging; self-esteem; self-actualization; the desire to know; and the need for the aesthetic (that is beauty). If indeed these are the fundamental needs of humanity, I would like Mr. Maslow to know that our Christ can meet those needs. He meets the need of the physical, for he is a great provider; just ask the five thousand he fed on the hillside. He meets the need of safety, for he is our "refuge and strength"; just ask the disciples who were aboard the storm-tossed ship. He meets the need of love and acceptance, for he is the lover of our souls; just ask Mary Magdalene, out of whom he cast seven demons. He meets the need of a healthy self-esteem, for he showed us our worth by dying for us; just ask the Gadarene demoniac, whom Jesus left sitting clothed and in his right mind.

Chapter Ten

He meets the need of self-actualization, for he is our sanctifier who molds and shapes us through life's ups and downs; just ask Peter who went from being a cussin' fishermen to a converted fisher of men. He meets our need to know, for he is the Wisdom of God; just ask Nicodemus, whom Jesus engaged in a late-night seminar on soteriology and pneumatology. He meets our need for the aesthetic, for he is the essence of beauty; just ask the sister who anointed Jesus with the expensive perfume, whose life had been changed by the winsome spirit of our Lord. How can we be bored with one who can do all of that?

Christ meets humanity at the point of its deepest need. I do not mean to insult your intelligence with trivialities, but I must ask you a question: Have you gone to the store to buy toothpaste lately? It can be a traumatic experience. It can drive you crazy. It can take you an hour to pick up a tube of toothpaste! Why? It is because there are so many choices, and different kinds of toothpaste claim to offer different benefits. Once while I was shopping for toothpaste, one tube read "deep cleansing" toothpaste. Another said "extra-whitening" formula. I kept going and another read "fluoride protection". And then one read "breath freshening". I think there was one for those who had sensitive teeth and gums. Then yet another read "tartar control" formula. I was on the edge of despair until the Holy Ghost led me to a tube that simply said, "complete"! My troubles were over because this one could do it all. That's why I preach Jesus. That's why I can't be bored with him. He is Complete. No wonder the songwriter said, "None else could heal all our soul's diseases; no not one, no not one..."

The Content of Christocentric Preaching

What shall we say of our Lord? What is the core of the content of the kerygma which is the theological substratum from which our preaching emanates and to which it is eternally tied? John helps us in his inimitable prologue of John chapter one. John commences his gospel with a song of tribute to our Lord which summarizes the content of his gospel. He says, "And the Word was made flesh, and dwelt among us, (and we beheld his glory, as of the only begotten of the Father,) full of grace and truth." What words these are! He says, "And the Word was made flesh..." At the center of message is the

Chapter Ten

incarnation. The Word became flesh. The "logos" became "sarx". The mind of God, the very reason of God, became what we are. God became what we are that we might become more like God is! The Lord became what we were, but never stopped being what he was. "The omnipotent, in one instant, made himself breakable. He who was larger than the universe became an embryo. And he who sustains the world with a word chose to be dependent upon the nourishment of a young girl", so says Max Lucado. The Lord as a fetus! Majesty sleeping in a womb! The giver of life, being given life! How could we be bored with him? Incarnation is Jesus becoming what we are, and it is Jesus coming to where we are: "And the Word was made flesh and dwelt among us." He became "what" so that He could come "where." He could not have come to where we are, if he did not become what we are. In Jesus, God moved into the neighborhood. Jesus came from Heaven to the "hood." God, contrary to what the Greeks thought, did not deal with the world through intermediaries. God, in Jesus, actually moved in. This idea would be scandalous to the Greek mind, having been influenced by a quasi-gnosticism which contended that matter was evil, and therefore God had nothing to do with matter. The gospel, in its most fundamental form, is scandalous! But this is what we preach. We preach the incarnation. We preach that our Lord left "first class" to sit with those in "coach", so that those in "coach" could have reserved seats in first class.

And then John says in this song of tribute "And we beheld his glory…" At the center of our message is *crucifixion and resurrection*. He says, "and we beheld his glory." "Doxa" (glory) in John's theology was inclusive of the entire passion occurrence of Jesus. Glory was not just resurrection. Glory was also crucifixion. As Jesus stood on the threshold of the cross he said, "Now is the Son of Man glorified." Glory was not just in the victory of Sunday morning; but it was also in the pain of Friday evening. Sometimes your glory is in your crucifixion. Perhaps the Shekinah glory of God is most apparent during our most painful hours.

The Calvary event is at the core of our message. No matter how unpopular it may be, don't stop preaching the cross. The symbol of our faith is not the "dollar bill", it's the cross. We have to preach Calvary, because as I heard one man put it, "At that hill something eternally valid, forever decisive, and everlastingly sufficient took place." It was Gardner Taylor who said, "Something was done at Calvary which no preacher can ever describe and yet which no preacher can ever stop trying to describe. I'm not ashamed of it." "For I am not ashamed of the gospel of Jesus Christ; for it is the power of God unto Salvation..." (Romans 1:16, NKJV).

John concludes this verse by declaring "...full of grace and truth." At the core of our message is not only incarnation, crucifixion and resurrection, but also *"transformation."* Whatever Jesus is full of is the very thing that transforms broken humanity. He is full of it. What Christ is full of has to come out, because he is full of it. The word here for "full" (pleres) does not simply mean filled to capacity; it means filled beyond capacity, to the point that whatever it is can't contain what it is full of. Thus, whatever it is full of comes running out, and whatever is in the vicinity will be impacted by what is running out. Jesus has so much grace and truth that whoever is around Him will be impacted by grace and truth. Grace and truth overflow the banks and boundaries of his personhood. Whatever else we need, we need grace and truth. We need truth because we need to know what the standard is in this age of moral relativism. Indeed, we live with the remnants of what Kierkegaard called "the teleological suspension of the ethical". Therefore, we need some sense of objective truth. That truth is in Jesus. But we would be in trouble if all we had was truth. I need some grace to balance that truth because I don't always meet the standard. I've fallen short of the standard, over and over. But that is where grace picks me up. Some time ago I was sitting on the bench at the YMCA watching my daughter take swim lessons. In the water with her was a swim instructor showing her what she ought to be doing. If she wanted to keep from drowning, there was a certain way she had to swim. If she wanted to reach her destination, there was a certain way she had to swim. But I noticed that seated in an elevated chair above the pool was a lifeguard. The lifeguard was there just in case she missed the standard that the swim instructor had given her. The reason I'm not bored with Jesus is because he is the swim instructor who is full of truth; but he is also the lifeguard who is full of grace. Every Sunday the people need to hear of the One who is full of grace and truth!

Chapter Eleven

Unrolling the Scroll: Reclaiming Evangelical Preaching:

LUKE 4:16-20

If you want to know what a potato is really like you do not start by examining a French fry. You do not begin by analyzing a bowl of mashed potatoes. You do not begin with a bag of potato chips. You go back to a potato in its original form before it's been sliced, fried, mashed, or baked. When it comes to the word evangelical, we typically start with the French fry or the potato chip when seeking to understand it. In its potato chip form some people have unnecessarily eschewed it, and others have ignorantly embraced it.

On one hand, some circles in the Black Church tradition have shunned this designation because of what it is associated with. Some of us contend that to be called "evangelical" is diametrically opposed to being a liberationist. You cannot be an evangelical and a liberationist simultaneously is the is the thought of some thinkers, theologians and preachers within African American Christianity. So-called progressives stay away from the term "evangelical" as though it is the plague. This is unfortunate because since the establishment of the ante-bellum slave church in the South and the independent black churches of the North, the notion of "evangelicalism" has been most fully embodied by Black preachers and the Black church in America. I agree with Gayraud Wilmore who argues that throughout history we have witnessed the *deradicalization*

Chapter Eleven

of the Black church and the dechristianization of Black radicalism (Black Religion and Black Radicalism, p. 135). That notwithstanding, Black Christians have represented the idea of true evangelicalism for some time. According to the late Dr. Charles Booth, "Black preaching itself, has embodied evangelicalism that was biblically sound, intellectually resourceful and socially responsible" (*Bridging the Breach*, p. 96). It is therefore unfortunate that some of us have shunned the term evangelical simply because of association, instead of embracing it based on its actual meaning.

On the other hand, there are those who have ignorantly embraced it. I do not mean "ignorantly" in a pejorative sense. I mean "ignorant" in the fullest sense of being uninformed. "Evangelical" is an explosive, radical idea that some have glibly and naively taken hold of without considering its true meaning. There have been those in some strands of American Christianity who have claimed to be evangelical who may not know exactly what it means to be evangelical. American evangelicalism is a river fed by the confluence of three tributary streams: the sixteenth century reformation; eighteenth century revivalism; and nineteenth and twentieth century fundamentalism which was at odds with the modernists. The reformation emphasized "Christus solas", Christ alone, as opposed to Christ plus anything. Revivalism accentuated the personal conversion of the soul. Fundamentalism held to the inerrant authority of scripture.

These three tributaries led to varied and sometimes strange shapes of American evangelicalism. In the 1940s American evangelicalism took the form of the Billy Graham phenomenon. George Marsden says that "Anyone who liked Billy Graham was considered an evangelical" (*Understanding Fundamentalism and Evangelicalism*, p. 6). From the Billy Graham phenomenon, evangelicalism became embodied by the Southern Baptist Convention. During the 1950s and 1960s, the Southern Baptist convention confiscated the idea of "evangelical" and made it synonymous with its denominational identity. Jerry Falwell and the Moral Majority took hold of "evangelical" in the 1970s and 1980s and began to associate evangelicalism with patriotism. To be true to God was to be true to America.

Chapter Eleven

The flag and the cross were running neck and neck for spiritual allegiance. In Nazi Germany it was the swastika that eclipsed the cross; in Moral Majority America, the flag eclipsed the cross. Falwell and the Moral Majority connected evangelicalism to then President Ronald Reagan. The baton of evangelicalism was handed off to the Charismatic Movement during the 1980s and 1990s. Some leaders and churches of the Charismatic Movement had been influenced by the notion of "dispensational premillennialism" which deemphasized involvement in social causes. In this branch of the Charismatic Movement, **Pentecostalism and patriotism got married**, and the likes of Oral Roberts, Jimmy Swaggart, Jim Bakker and Pat Robertson performed the ceremony. Most recently, evangelicalism has been abducted by and taken shape within the Trump cult which sees abortion and same sex relationships as the only social issues that merit Christian attention.

It is understandable why some Christians, and particularly Black preachers and churches have been reticent about embracing the term "evangelical." The term has been abused, misused and confused. The term has been sullied and tainted. But I contend that it is time to reclaim "evangelical." It is time to reclaim evangelical preaching. Perhaps it is time to "take it back" and restore the idea to its original meaning and purpose. The reason this is essential is because evangelical preaching is the key to transforming the kingdoms of this world into the kingdom of our God. Evangelical preaching is what will empower people to be "more than conquerors" in this current *seitz im Leben*. Preaching the evangel is the key to lifting people above their current fears.

Jesus defines what it means to be an evangelical in Luke 4 both by what he says and what he does. Jesus "unrolls the scroll", and by doing so he reinforces the idea of what it means to be an evangelical and what it means to do evangelical preaching.

What Jesus says and does in this passage reveals that evangelicalism is characterized by *an authentic confidence in scriptures*. Jesus comes to his hometown of Nazareth. When he arrives, he affirms the Sabbath, Synagogue, and the Scriptures. He goes to the Synagogue on the Sabbath and while there he reads the scriptures. As revolutionary as Jesus was, he operated within the confines of his Jewish tradition. He affirmed the Sabbath. It was his worship day and so he goes to church. Jesus believed in "sacred time" The Sabbath was sacred time, so he goes to church.

On the Sabbath he goes to the synagogue. The synagogue, at that time, was void of much salvific activity, yet Jesus went anyway. Not only did he believe in sacred time, he also believed in sacred space. He went, according to the narrator, "as was his custom." The only other time in the Gospels that we read of Jesus doing anything according to his custom was when he went to the garden to pray.

At some point during the worship experience, Jesus was handed the scroll of Isaiah. The Ruler of the synagogue invites Jesus to read and comment on the scripture. Jesus stood up, he was given the scroll, and then he unrolled it. Jesus intentionally chooses this passage in Isaiah. He wants to show that he has a messianic consciousness. He reads this passage which, in the words of Charles Booth, is his "declaration of intent" and his "ministry manifesto."

Jesus unrolls the scroll. The verb "unrolls" was borrowed from the medical world and had to do with the opening up of various body parts where life was stored. Jesus has such high regard for scriptures, that he unrolls it and bases his ministry on it. The job of every preacher is to unroll the scroll. Our job is not to add content to what's on the scroll; our job is to unroll it. There is already enough written on the scroll, our job is to unroll it to the best of our ability.

Real evangelicalism has high regard for scriptures as the final authority in matters of faith, living, and ethics. The bible, properly understood in context, is central. The primary concern is not in the areas of inerrancy and infallibility. Those are important matters to many of us. However, the real concern is the authority of scriptures as the revealed Word of God. As Jesus is the incarnate Word, and as preaching is the spoken Word of God; the scriptures are the written Word of God. Therefore, we approach the scripture with a level of reverence. Even as we engage in so-called literary, historical redaction, and contextual criticism, we do it with a level of reverence.

Chapter Eleven

We unroll the scroll because scripture is one of the sources of the preacher's power. Power may be absent sometimes because we unroll everything but the scroll. In Matthew 22:29, Jesus told the Pharisees, "You know not the scriptures, nor the power of God." There must be some relationship between scripture and power. Preachers are trustees of divine revelation, but it is difficult to be that if we do not have some confidence in the power of Word. John R.W. Stott tells the story of a travelling preacher who was passing through the security checkpoint at an airport. It was long before the days of electronic scanning, and the security officer was rummaging through the preacher's briefcase. He came across the black cardboard box which contained the preacher's Bible and was curious to discover its contents. "What's in that box?" he asked suspiciously. The preacher said, "Dynamite." The evangelical preacher believes that what is in his/her hand, is dynamite.

What Jesus does and says reveals that evangelicalism is characterized by an authentic confidence in scripture. It is also characterized by *a communication of the good news*. Jesus reads from Isaiah 61. "The Spirit of the Lord is upon me, because he has anointed me to preach..." The anointing is meant for service. The anointed does not brag on being anointed. The anointing is not an end in itself. It is meant for the empowerment of service, and particularly the service of preaching. Three times this scriptural reference says "preach." The word for "preach" in v. 18 is the word "euangelion." It means good news or glad tidings. The evangelical is the one who preaches good news. The word for preach in v.18b and v.19 is the word "kerruso." That word means to "herald." It is the image of the "town-crier" who comes with an urgent message. Jesus says he is both the good news and the herald of the good news. Jesus is the message and the messenger. He embodies what he announces; he announces what he embodies. "Euangelion" is the message of good news. "Kerruso" is the act of heralding that message.

Evangelical preaching heralds the good news. Jesus is the good news therefore Jesus spoke of himself. We proclaim Jesus since Jesus is the good news. We do it as heralds. We proclaim the good news the way that a play-by-play sports

Chapter Eleven

announcer announces a game. Have you ever noticed how excited the sports announcer gets when he/she is announcing a game? When a team scores a touchdown, the voice of the announcer rises to an enthusiastic crescendo. The tone and tenor of the announcer's voice matches what happens on the field. If something extraordinary happens on the field, it is reflected in the voice of the commentator. Something extraordinary happened in incarnation, our voices should match it. Something extraordinary happened in crucifixion, our voices should match it. Something extraordinary happened in resurrection, our voices should match it. The evangelical preacher is a herald of the good news.

Evangelical preachers communicate the good news of Jesus Christ because we believe that that is what leads to conversions and changed lives. Evangelical preaching does not apologize for attempting to get people "saved." We still believe in being "saved." "Saved, by His power divine. Saved to new life sublime! Life now is sweet and my joy is complete, for I am saved, saved, saved…" The language sounds archaic;

the language is associated with a brand of evangelicalism that we sometimes shun. However, the idea is yet true. The key to changing society is to change lives; the key to changing lives is to preach the good news. We stand in the shoes of Paul who said, "I am not ashamed of the gospel of Jesus Christ, for it is the power of God unto salvation." The proclamation of Jesus Christ is the bridge that gets people to salvation. The proclamation of Jesus Christ is the "unto" that transports people to this thing called salvation. The "euangelion" is God's "unto." This idea is at the core of evangelical preaching. I was driving Dr. Mack King Carter, and he said to me, "Jerry, unfortunately most preachers are more interested in sermonizing than they are in proclaiming the kerygma." Sermonizing is what tickles our ears, but proclamation of the kerygma is what leads to changed lives!

Jesus' actions and words in this passage reveal that evangelical preaching is characterized by an authentic confidence in the scriptures; it is characterized by a communication of the good news, and it is characterized by *a commitment to liberation*. Here's where some of the traditional evangelicals get off the bus. American

Chapter Eleven

evangelicalism is comfortable with a confidence in scripture. It is at home with a communication of the good news, but it leaves us when we start talking the liberation of the oppressed.

Jesus says that he has been sent to proclaim and to be the good news to the poor, to the captives, to the blind and to the oppressed. The "poor" is a reference to those who are impoverished because of systems that are rigged against them. There are systems in place that are meant to increase the wealth of the wealthy and to increase the poverty of the impoverished. The captive is a reference to anybody who is enslaved to anything that prevents them from becoming what they were created to be. It is the modern-day equivalent of "addiction." The "blind" refers to those who are physically sick and infirmed. The "oppressed" can also be translated "the bruised." The bruised refers to those who have been "broken like shattered pottery." Jesus says he has come for the impoverished, for the addicted, for the sick, and for the broken.

Any church that does not aim some ministry and activism on behalf of these parties is not evangelical. Preaching that does not address these parties is not evangelical. Woven into the fabric of evangelicalism is liberation. You cannot be evangelical and only be concerned about life in the womb, but not concerned about life outside of the womb. Dr. Charles Booth was right in his book when he said that "Any gospel which is not social is not Gospel…In the incarnation the gospel became social." In the incarnation, the spiritual and the social were inextricably bound. The Word becoming flesh is a social event. Those who refuse to connect justice to preaching and ministry should stop using the term "evangelical." "Evangelical" is an explosive, revolutionary term.

Jesus informs us that you cannot be evangelical and be silent about the poor, the enslaved, the infirmed, and the oppressed. In her book *Caste*, Isabel Wilkerson speaks of the "Evil of Silence". She says that as Jewish bodies were being incinerated:

> The ash rose from the crematorium into the air, and was carried by karma and breeze, and settled onto the front steps and geranium beds of the townspeople living outside the

gates of death at Sachsenhausen, north of Berlin. The ash coated the swing sets and paddling pools in the backyards of the townspeople. (p. 90)

The townspeople, who were aware of what was happening, simply swept the ash off of their porches. They swept the ash from their porches! Evangelicalism that does not speak to and that does not speak for the classes of people identified by Isaiah and Jesus, does the same thing; it simply sweeps the ash off of the porch. And to them Dietrich Bonhoeffer says, "Silence in the face of evil is itself evil…God will not hold us guiltless. Not to speak is to speak. Not to act is to act."

Jesus challenges those who call themselves evangelicals to take action "today." He says, "Today, this scripture is fulfilled." **The first public word of the adult Jesus is, "Today."** Justice for the poor is for today. Attention for the sick is for today. Deliverance for the addicted is for today. Wholeness for the broken is for today. God's time is always today. For Jesus, today is never allowed to become yesterday or someday; it's always today.

Jesus defines "evangelical" by what he says and what he does. According to Jesus, evangelicalism asserts an authentic confidence in scripture; it communicates the good news; it is committed to liberation; and it is *in conflict with the status quo.* Jesus' reading and sermon on this day in the synagogue gets him into trouble. By the time it's all over, the townspeople are ready to throw him off of a cliff. They cannot tolerate this Jesus. Cultural evangelicalism has a hard time with Jesus. The temptation is to throw him off the cliff and create another Jesus who is more "red-blooded" American. The Jesus of cultural evangelicalism is an idol.

They are angry with Jesus because Jesus implied that God's favor flows to those outside of Nazareth. They are mad at Jesus because Jesus refuses to limit God's favor and blessing to a particular group. They are troubled by his inclusion of the marginalized in the economy of God's kingdom. They feel like God's blessings are limited to people who look like, believe like, and think like them. So, they become angry with Jesus because he upsets the status quo. Real evangelicalism finds it difficult to sleep with certain political parties. It doesn't rest well with the status quo. The crowd in church becomes angry with Jesus to the point of violence. Anger and violence are the last defense by those who have been made to face the truth of their own bigotry. This is the crowd that storms the Capitol. This is the crowd that forms itself in mobs.

It is this mob's intent to take the life of Jesus. "But Jesus passed through the midst of them and went on his way." God takes care of those who are true to the evangel! Jesus "passed through" his trouble. He did not have to go around it. He goes through it. God's favor enables you to get through what others have to get around. Harry Houdini tops the list of the most famous escape artists in history. Houdini has gotten out of some places from which no one has ever been able to escape. Houdini made it out of the "Chinese Water Torture Cell" and the "Milk Can." Houdini died on Halloween, 1926 and we have not heard from him since. Perhaps the name Jesus should be placed above Houdini as the greatest escape artist. He was able to escape the clutches of Herod as a baby. He was able to escape and get through this crowd that wanted to kill him.

Just like Houdini, Jesus died. Houdini, however, is still in the grave. Jesus was raised and is alive forevermore. Reclaim that!

Chapter Twelve

A Pregnant Silence: Disconnecting in Order to Connect

1 KINGS 19:9-18

In Victor Hugo's *Notre-Dame de Paris* (a play set in 1482, when printing presses were just getting established in Louis XI's France), Archdeacon Claude Frollo sees his first printed book and marvels at its production quality. He stands near

Notre-Dame and, looking up at the cathedral, says, "Ceci tuera cela" (this will kill that). The Archdeacon laments what would become of the hierarchical authority of the Catholic church and the role and prominence of oral transmission because of the accessibility of information through the printed word. The printing press which Johannes Gutenberg invented in 1950 revolutionized society for the good; but it also cost society something.

For our generation it's not the printing press, it's the smartphone, it's the Internet, it's Instagram, it's Facebook, it's Periscope, it's emailing, it's texting, it's calling. As much as these mediums have revolutionized communication, they have also cost us something. Ceci tuera cela. "This has killed that." In his book, *The End of Absence*, Michael Harris contends, "Every revolution in communication technology is as much an opportunity to be drawn away from something as it is to be drawn toward something." He goes on, "As we embrace technology's gifts, we usually fail to consider what they ask from us in return- the subtle, hardly noticeable payments we make in exchange for their marvelous service." The monthly payment you make for your smartphone is not all that device costs. Technology not only brings gifts, it also comes with a price. Indeed, technology draws us toward something, but it also draws us away from something.

The ubiquitous usage and influence of devices and social media hides the costs. Inventions like the printing press and the smartphone are more than discreet gadgets; they dissolve into the very atmosphere of our lives. Most of us are "digital immigrants". We journeyed into the digital age. Many of our children and grandchildren are and will be "digital natives". They were born into this age. Immigrants take notice of the new country versus the old one from which they have come. Natives don't notice because what they have is all they've known. Natives do not know of a time when there were no cell phones and smartphones. We now breathe the very air of technological influence. By 2012, we were asking Google to help us find things more than a trillion times each year in 146 languages. We were also sending one another 144 billion emails – every day. In 2013, we "liked" 4.5 billion items on Facebook every day. That same year, we uploaded one hundred hours of video to YouTube for every minute of real time. Every second, we uploaded 637 photos to Instagram. Worldwide there are now 6.8 billion cell phone subscriptions. According to Nielsen, the average teenager now manages upward of four thousand text messages every month.

The statistics go on and on which indicate the pervasive use of technology in communication. These communicative mediums have positively impacted every facet of human society, including the church. The history of human knowledge is now at our fingertips. You can tweet pithy and powerful sayings to people right now. We can send images to folks in faraway places. Before I get off the plane, I can inform friends and loved ones that I have safely landed. But at what cost? I wonder, has "this" killed "that."? In *The End of Absence*, Harris argues that all of this technological "presence" has ended the possibility of absence. You can never be absent anymore. As I'm writing this right now, I'm checking my text messages every fifteen minutes, because I can't afford to be absent for too long. We have, in the words of Michael Harris, "experienced the end of absence –the

Chapter Twelve

loss of lack." The daydreaming silences in our lives are filled; the burning solitudes are extinguished. "This" has killed "that." This has killed absence. This has killed solitude. This has killed silence. This has killed focus.

In a very real sense, "this" (the communicative revolution via smartphones and social media) has not only killed absence, it has killed real presence. Texting provides a way of "communicating" without really needing to be present. When we don't want to be alone and yet don't want the hassle that fellow humans represent either, the digital filter is an ideal compromise. The smartphone is itself a far, far safer friend than a messy, unpredictable human. It is so much more comfortable to be on a train gazing into my phone as though anthropomorphically it has become human, than it is to actually engage a human being next to me. And have you noticed that we are much bolder in a text than we are in face to face conversation. There are some things you will say in text that you won't say personally. We are a part of a population which is more at ease with technologies than with one another.

The question remains, has "this" killed "that"? It is difficult for us to be present anywhere because we are trying to be present everywhere. It's hard to be present in any one moment, because we are attempting to be present actually and virtually. We can't be present in worship because we are texting and tweeting. I understand the purpose of getting information out, as long as we know what we are giving up. I observe some of the gatherings I am part of with my friends. We will converse sporadically- in between time on our phones. No one is ever totally present because we can't be absent from the world. There is this insatiable desire to be in contact with the world around us. The problem is the carnage of constant connection. "This kills that."

A desire to be constantly connected has disconnected us from the discipline of solitude and silence. I call it a discipline because Richard Foster calls it such in *Celebration of Discipline*. "Solitude" is a corporate discipline that has to be nurtured. Anything that is a discipline is something that does not come naturally. It does not come naturally because many of us are afraid of silence. Silence is an endangered species. Silence is awkward. We fill those nagging moments of silence with television, radio, and frivolous conversation. Why are we so afraid of it? Could it be that we hear things that we'd rather not hear when there is too much silence? Could it be that the restlessness of troubled spirits is more pronounced in those moments of quiet? In the silence and solitude, I can no longer run from me. My anxieties and fears stare me in the face. Emptiness taps me on the shoulder. Anthony Campolo says, "We make noise on New Year's Eve so that we don't have to hear the grass growing over our graves." I have to do something in non-active moments so that I don't have to dialogue with memory. This is why I must be constantly connected. God forbid I am somewhere where I can't get a "connection."

As intimidating as silence and solitude can be, they are necessary in order to be human. Silence can be pregnant with possibilities. Elijah's strange encounter with the Holy teaches us this. Elijah, as the preacher, before he stands before the people, is engulfed by a pregnant silence. Right in the shadow of the victory of Mount Carmel, Elijah is now fearful, frustrated and depressed. He and his servant journey to Beersheba. He gets as far away from his assignment as possible. Elijah is as far from his assignment as he can venture. He leaves his servant in Beersheba, and he goes further into the wilderness. He has given up on living and decides to park under a broom brush. He prays, what he believes to be his last prayer: I'm done. Here's my ordination papers, I'm done. Here's my letter of resignation. I've had enough. Here's my clergy vestments. I'm done. I've had enough of this… The angel taps him on the shoulder and rains on his pity party. "Get up and eat," says the angel. The angel does not tell him to attend a new conference; just to get up and eat. Elijah gets up and sees that what is necessary for strength has been provided. He eats and goes to sleep.

He now has not enough strength to journey further, and he makes it to Mount Horeb, also known as Mount Sinai. He had been in a Mount Carmel season, now he is in a Mount Horeb season. Ministry can have you in either season! Those who have done ministry for any amount of time, know something about Carmel and Horeb. Mount Carmel is where you called down fire, and were victorious over the prophets of Baal. Horeb is where you enter a cave and don't want to

Chapter Twelve

come out. On Mount Carmel everyone is singing your praises; on Mount Horeb you don't want to be bothered with anyone. If you are going to have staying power in life and in ministry, you have to know how to negotiate between Carmel and Horeb. The irony is that it does not take long to go from Carmel to Horeb. You can be on Carmel Sunday morning, and Horeb Sunday night. All it takes is one church meeting to land you on Horeb. Elijah ends up in Horeb/Sinai. Sinai was a paradoxical place to end up. On one hand, this was the hallowed ground of divine encounter. It was there the presence of the Lord descended. It was there where the glory of the Lord knocked the people off of their feet. It was there where Moses communed with Jehovah and received the law for the people. In spite of such a sacred, storied history, this was also a desolated, quiet place. It was surrounded by barrenness.

It was in this place that Elijah discovers how pregnant with power silence can be. Silence can't be taken for granted. Quietness does not mean weakness. There is a real power in silence. My grandmother, Helen Jackson, had two dogs at one time. She had a loud Chihuahua, named "Prince" and a quiet Doberman, named "King".

The loud bark of the Chihuahua was not an indication of strength, because it was harmless. The quiet demeanor of the Doberman was not an indication of weakness, because it would eat you up! I'd much rather tangle with that Chihuahua making all that noise, than I would with that silent Doberman.

> Some of God's greatest works are carried on in silence:
>
> Noiselessly the planets move in their orbits; their voice cannot be heard as they sweep through their appointed paths in space. No sound attends the crystallization of the dewdrops on the myriad blades of grass in the summer evenings, and while crops are growing in the fields, so profound is the stillness that nature seems to be asleep. How quiet it is each dawn when the moon says good-bye and relinquishes the throne to the hello of the sun!

Elijah is engulfed by a pregnant silence. With what was this silence pregnant? More than anything, this rapturous moment was pregnant with **an encounter with a presence**. This silence

Chapter Twelve

was pregnant so it could allow for **an encounter with a presence**. The Lord finds Elijah in a cave and tells him to go stand at the mouth of the cave, because the Lord is about to pass by. He is not, in this case, an abiding presence; the Lord is a passing presence, because that's all Elijah can take right now. As Elijah approaches the opening of the cave, a powerful wind passes by, but the Lord is not in all that noise. Then an earthquake rocks the mountain, but the Lord was not in all of that chaos. Then a fire engulfs the mountain, but God was not in all that excitement. You would have expected God to be in the wind. After all, when the Lord was trying to seize Job's undivided attention, he spoke to Job out of the whirlwind. You would have expected the Lord to come in the earthquake. The last time that the Lord descended upon Mount Sinai in the presence of the Israelites, there was an earthquake that measured high on the Richter scale. You would have expected the Lord to be in the fire, because when the Lord was trying to get the attention of Moses, he came through the theophany of the burning bush. But since we can't control how God will manifest, God comes at Elijah in an unexpected way.

After all of that, Elijah hears the sound of silence. There was a sheer silence that cut through the noise and commotion. The silence made more noise than the wind, the earthquake, and the fire. It caused a deeper disturbance. Because it contradicted all that Elijah had heretofore been experiencing. For some time now, Elijah's life had been characterized by action, crowds, and noise. Even Elijah's temperament was fiery and enthusiastic. Thus, that which was the opposite of his personality would be the only thing that would shock him into full attention. Elijah was used to the miraculous: being fed by birds, filling empty barrels and jars, raising a boy from the dead, calling fire down on Carmel, and rain down from heaven. He was used to the extraordinary, yet this time only the ordinary would get his attention. It would have been quicker and easier for God to have been in the wind, earthquake, or fire. But hearing God's voice sometimes requires a longer attention span than that.

And that is exactly what happened. The writer does not even say that the Lord was in the silence. However, he does say that right after this experience of silence the Lord spoke to him. The sound of the silence prepared Elijah for an encounter with the "mysterium tremendum." Silence might not always contain a divine encounter, but it at least prepares you for it. Elijah had to disconnect from the noise of his surroundings in order to connect with the Holy...

There is a call on the life of the preacher to spend some time in silence and solitude. Long before the internet, long before smartphones, Dietrich Bonhoeffer wrote in, *Life Together*:

> Let him who cannot be alone beware of community. Alone you stood before God when he called you; alone you had to answer that call; alone you had to struggle and pray; and alone you will die and give an account to God. You cannot escape from yourself; for God has singled you out. If you refuse to be alone you are rejecting Christ's call to you, and you can have no part in the community of those who are called.

There is a call on the life of the preacher to enter into the silence and stillness of reflection. The moments of solitude help to center us. You can't just rush in from the "streets", open up your Bible, and expect revelation. It takes getting centered.

Silence has a way of purging you. Preaching, in the words of Dr. Ralph West, is born of silence. It comes from the inside out. It takes silence and stillness to brood over a passage of scripture. It takes silence to hear the voice of God through the text. The preaching event is not organically located in the reading of commentaries or in doing exegetical work. It finds its roots in "blessed quietness". The call on the preacher is to disconnect in order to connect. We do not want it said that "this has killed that".

Chapter Thirteen

Overflow Preaching: "Go Get it, Eat it, and Preach it"

REVELATION 10:8-11

As preachers we open our mouths so much. We're always called on to say something. We open up our mouths to preach; teach; counsel; lead meetings; give remarks; install; ordain; consecrate; marry people; bury people and so on. We always have something to say. And we're always called on to say something. It's woven into the very fabric of our calling: we are "heralds" and by nature heralds "say something." I have to admit, I do get tired of it sometimes. I get tired of always having to say something. I recently rebelled. We had a Black History program at our church, and the committee put me on to do "closing remarks" (there's always closing remarks). I didn't have any closing remarks. So I just said, "No". It was a wonderful service, but I just had nothing to say; so, I didn't. If you have nothing to say; don't say anything. It's bad to have nothing to say, and still try to say something.

Since we are always called on to say something, especially in the area of preaching, it pays to have something on the inside, so that we do have something to say. It's disconcerting to be called on to say something, and have nothing to say. There's an old book by William Stidger entitled *Preaching Out of the Overflow*. Stidger opens this book by telling the story about day he was riding on a train through the oil fields of Kansas. As he gazed at the fields, he noticed that there were three types of oil wells: dry holes, wells that have to be pumped, and wells that overflow. Dry holes are those in which there is no oil flowing. Stidger says

Chapter Thirteen

that there are preachers like that. There is an emptiness on the inside because nothing has been stored there, thus when it comes time to preach, there is nothing to say. Second, there are wells that have to be pumped. Those are wells which are able to produce some oil, but you have to work hard to get any oil. These are preachers who come up with sermons, but they are born of sweat and drudgery. It's a job trying to find something to say. You almost get sick because Sundays seem to come before sermons. And then, according to Stidger, there are wells that are overflowing with oil. When it's time to produce oil, there is little difficulty because the subterranean flow of oil gives birth to easy production above ground.

The best preaching is that preaching which flows from the abundance of what has been stored away. The key to "overflow preaching" is preparation. Don't take it for granted, because sermon preparation often gets swallowed up in the quagmire of other pastoral, denominational, ecclesiastical, and personal responsibilities. But no matter how busy we are, we must understand that our priority is preaching. And since preaching is our priority, then preparation is our priority. There is no effective preaching without preparation. The late Caesar Clark was right, "Limited time in study, results in wasted time in the pulpit." Although the image and role of the 21st century pastor has changed; and although we need to be astute in areas of finance, technology, and business, we must never forget that our priority is preaching. When Jesus came, Jesus came preaching. When it comes down to it, preaching is the priority of the pastor! The one thing you've been called to do in your congregation, which no one else has been called to do, is to preach.

Overflow preaching requires two types of preparation: long haul and short haul; advanced and immediate. Long haul preparation is the preparation we do daily, even before we have our assignment. It is the reading, praying, and observing we do as lifestyle discipline. John Broadus says, "All of a minister's past study, all of his/her reading, meditation, prayer, all pastoral administration, all observant contacts with the world of people and things contribute to the groundwork and superstructure of every sermon." According to Cleophus LaRue, "Overflow preachers preach from a wealth of materials, knowledge, disciplined insight and

Chapter Thirteen

rich experience gained from diligent study and conscious reflection on God's presence in the world." There is a difference between preparing for preaching and preparing to preach. Preparing for preaching is what we do perpetually; preparing to preach a particular sermon is what we do week to week. There used to be a few brothers who are members of my church who happen to play for the New York Jets. One particular week they were preparing to play the New England patriots in a huge game. I stopped one of them in Bible Study and asked him if they were ready. He said, "We've done most of our preparation in the heat of summer while no one was looking. From week to week all we do is game plan for a particular opponent." As preachers, when we put in our training camp time when no one is looking, all we have to do is game plan from week to week.

Overflow preaching results in having more than what you need to preach. You cannot say it all in one sermon. Overflow preaching knows what needs to be included in a sermon and what needs to be omitted. The amateur tries to crowd everything in, the professional knows what to leave out. Overflow preaching skims off the top of what you have stored in your soul and in your mind. You don't need to include everything you've studied in the sermon. If you are baking a cake, you might go to the store and buy a dozen eggs. You might buy a 5lb bag of sugar. You might buy a bottle of oil. But you don't use all of that in the baking of a single cake. You may be able to use some of the content in the containers later when you bake another cake. It takes a disciplined mind to know what not to include in the sermon. We should believe in an economy of words, so that we don't "over-word" our preaching. The last thing you should do before you preach, is to go through the sermon and take out what you don't need instead of adding something.

Overflow preaching recognizes the need of a homiletic mind. A homiletic mind is a mind that views the common with the eye of a preacher and sees in the common what others do not see. The homiletic mind, in the words of Shakespeare, "sees sermons in the stones." Jesus had a homiletic mind. He saw sheep, soil and seeds, fish, wheat and tares, goats, yeast, treasure, and coins like no one else did. The homiletic mind is on the look-out for preaching insight and illustration. Preachers are hunters and gatherers. It's not an obsession, it's a consciousness. We

Chapter Thirteen

don't look at nature the same way. We don't go to the movies and the theater the same way. We don't go in and out of airports the same way. We don't view relationships the same way. We don't look at technology the same way. I don't even look at sporting events the same way. The homiletic mind "notices." Preachers have to notice. We can't be in a hurry like everyone else. In the words of the late Frederick Sampson of Detroit, "we have to take time to take time." The homiletic mind notices, and then preaches from the overflow of what we notice. I notice the Blue Jay in my backyard, which sings no matter what the weather is like. Robert Smith says that "Preachers have to live in the world as tourists and not as residents." In New York City, in the Times Square area, you can tell the difference between tourists and residents. Residents are walking just trying to make it from one place to another. Tourists notice everything around them. There is a wonder and amazement about that which residents take for granted.

We preach from the overflow of what?

1. We preach from the overflow of a life in the Spirit. Sitting still before and with God stirs our souls to the point where it provides overflow. This requires investment in solitude. Ralph West says, "Preaching is not born of noise, it's born of silence." When we spend time in the presence of God, where we have the opportunity to nurture life in the Spirit, people will come to the same conclusion about us that they did concerning Peter and John, "… they've been with Jesus."

2. We preach from the overflow of a knowledge of Scriptures. Someone asked Gardner Taylor what he would have done differently in ministry; he said he would have read the Bible more and prayed more. Read the scripture devotionally and not just vocationally. Elie Wiesel, the Holocaust survivor, theologian, and philosopher, says that "The Rabbi who loves the Torah, and subsequently reads it, actually crawls into the cranium of Yahweh." To spend time in scriptures is to crawl into the cranium (mind) of God and come out with

thoughts of the Mysterium Tremendum. We can preach from the overflow of that experience.

3. We preach from the overflow of insight from the scholars. Read everything you can. One preacher challenged a group of preachers at a conference to read a book a week. One of the brothers stood up and said, "The average preacher doesn't have time to read a book a month." To that the speaker said, "That's why you will always be average preachers!"

4. We preach from the overflow of the observation of society. Karl Barth was right, "We ought to have the Bible in one hand and the newspaper in the other hand." Thumb through newspapers and magazines and cut out articles. Go online and read what's happening around us.

5. We preach from the overflow of our experience with the Saints. Pay close attention to administration and visitations. Each week we should be in the valley with the people so that we can assess the condition of the dry bones.

6. We preach from the overflow of fellowship with other soldiers. Develop relationships with preachers who are not just talking about foolishness. It is true that "iron sharpens iron."

In this passage John was, in a real sense, challenged to preach from the overflow. The Apostle John was exiled to the rocky isle of Patmos. John is on this island being prepared for an assignment. God can prepare you even when you're in exile. Exile is preparation. John's church needed a word. The Book of Revelation is really about what God shows the preacher; so that the preacher would have something to say to the people. The heavens keep being opened up, so that John could see what the people did not see so that he could say what the people needed to hear. For John there was no saying until there was some seeing. The preacher is a seer first and a "sayer" second. No "seeing", no "saying"!

John looks up in this chapter, and sees a strong angel. The angel is a messenger who has something to give John. The angel has one foot on land and one on the sea. God owns all of it. You can put your foot on what you own! This angel

Chapter Thirteen

has something in his hand. He has a book. This book is for the preacher. John is commanded to do three things with this book.

He is commanded to *go get it*. Access the book. The angel says to John, "Go get the book..." The truth of this book is available to the preacher. It is accessible. The angel does not want John to have to make up something to say. John is not to come up with any special revelation for that season. The angel only wants John to say, what has been said. If it has not been said, then John can't say it. We have to be careful with all of this new revelation. When you have exhausted all that has been said in the book, then you can come up with your own revelation. Integrity in prophetic preaching is about saying what has been said. What has been said is enough!

This book which is accessible, is open. It is an open book. The last time there was any mention of a book and a strong angel in Revelation, it was in Rev. 5 when the one on the throne had a sealed book. The angel asked, "Who is worthy to open the book..." No one was found, and John wept. The Elder said, "Don't weep, for the lion of the tribe of Judah has prevailed to open the book." Jesus, the Lion and Lamb, took the book amid adoring shouts of the heavenly hosts and opened it. Jesus' redemptive act has provided access to the book. That's why it is "open" in this passage. Jesus died so that we could preach from this open book.

"Go get it" is the command. The angel is not going to drop the truth of the book in the preacher's lap. What is in it, the preacher has to go get. Read it- go get it! Meditate on it- go get it! Read the Greek and Hebrew, if you can (or at least read the helps) - go get it! Read the commentaries- go get it! Brood over it- go get it! It is open, but you have to go get it, in order to receive what is in it!

Something strange happens in this passage. When John is told to go get the book, the word used for "book" is the word "book." It is the word for a complete scroll. That's in v.8. When John goes to get it in v.10, it literally reads, "...and I took the booklet." He is told to get the book, the full scroll. But when he gets into to book, he only comes away with a booklet." None of us, no matter how good you are, can get the whole book. Sunday after Sunday, I don't care

Chapter Thirteen

how gifted you are, all we present are "booklets" derived from the book. The open book is what we are presented with, the little book is what we manage to get a hold of. This cuts across all hubris and pride, because no matter how much they shout; no matter how much we "killed the house", just know that it was just a booklet. You have to go back to the book to get another booklet for the coming Sunday.

And then John is commanded to *eat it!* After you go get it; eat it. There by the river Chebar, Ezekiel was commanded to do the same thing. Eat it! Assimilate it into your muscles and tissues. Eat it, because you are what you eat, and, says the Lord, I want you to become what you need to say. There should be no existential space between my being and my saying. What I am saying needs to be a part of me, so that I am not delivering some disembodied lecture or treatise, but that I am preaching from the very overflow of what I have consumed. If I am preaching from 2 Cor. 12 where Paul declares that "His grace is sufficient..." I need to eat that until I feel it. I heard singer Jennifer Hudson say in a television interview that she rehearses a song over and over until it becomes her. That's what we do with the Word! Rehearse it until it becomes YOU!

Now you can't eat it if you wait until Saturday night. The best you can do if you wait until the last minute to prepare is just sniff it. But you can't get full from just sniffing the word. That could be why I go to the pulpit empty sometimes.

When I eat it, it will be sweet to the mouth but bitter to the stomach. Preaching involves bitters and sweets. There are the sweets of "Amens" and the bitters of indifferent faces. There are the sweets of the excitement of standing; there are the bitters of reading, outlining, and writing. Some of you know about the bitters and sweets of ministry. This is what James Massey might call "The Burdensome Joy of Preaching." The word was bitter in John's stomach because it may have been a word of judgment, which did not sit well with the preacher. The word is sweet to the mouth and bitter to the stomach because the mouth is where the word is supposed to be. Jeremiah said "It's like fire in my bones…" But that was because he had shut his mouth! The mouth is the place where the word is vented and voiced. The word is not meant for the belly. And thus it makes the belly sick until it gets to the mouth. "I said I wasn't gonna' tell nobody, but I couldn't keep it to myself!"

Chapter Thirteen

Finally, John is told to *preach it!* You don't eat the book just to get full. You eat it so that you can feed. You dine so that you can declare. You sit at the table so that you can stand in the pulpit. Notice there is no preaching it until you have gone to get it and have eaten it. Sometimes I'm so anxious to say it, that I neglect going to get it and eating it. My preaching will become anorexic if I don't get it and eat it, before I say it. And anorexic preaching produces anorexic churches. "Prophesy to the peoples, the nations, the tongues, and kings." In each case the assignment gets more prestigious. First before your own people; then in foreign places (flying all over the place); and then prophesy before kings, that is to say, in the presence of important people. It is a great assignment. But there is to be none of that, until you "go get it" and "eat it." Before we stand anywhere, our prayer is that God might fill us. We need to be filled daily because all of us are like the man who kept going to every revival in town in order to be "filled". In his own words, "All of us leak." Trouble will cause you to leak. Sin causes us to leak...That's why we ask God to fill us afresh each time we stand. We can't do it alone, fill us! The faces are sometimes cold, fill us! I need your presence Lord, fill us! The assignment is too difficult fill us! We need to ask God for this fresh filling over and over. Our prayer is "Fill my cup Lord. I lift it up Lord. Come and quench this thirsting in my soul…"

Chapter Fourteen

Standing in the Assembly: A Reconsideration of the Place and Future of Preaching

One day while Chicken Little was walking in the woods, an acorn falls from a tree and hits the top of her little head. "My, oh, my, the sky is falling. I must run and tell the lion about it," said Chicken

Little and she begins to run. She runs and runs. By and by she meets the hen. "Where are you going?" asks the hen. "Oh, Henny Penny, the sky is falling, and I am going to tell the lion about it. "How do you know it?" asks Henny Penny. "It hit me on the head, so I know it must be so", says Chicken little. So, the two run until they meet Ducky Lucky. "The sky is falling," says Henny Penny. "How do you know?" asks Ducky Lucky. "It hit Chicken Little on the head." The three of them run until they run into Foxy Loxy. "Where are you going?" asks Foxy Loxy. "The sky is falling and we're going to tell the lion." says Ducky Lucky. "Do you know where he lives?" asks Foxy Loxy. "We don't," said Chicken Little, Henny Penny, and Ducky Lucky. Foxy Loxy says, "Come with me, I'll show you." They follow Foxy Loxy. Foxy Loxy says, "Here is his den, walk on in…" Chicken Little, Henny Penny, and Ducky Lucky walk in, and they never make it out. [emphasis added]

About twenty or thirty years ago an acorn fell from the tree of traditional Christian preaching and hit a few homiletic and theological minds on the head, and since then, the rumor is that the sky of Christian preaching is falling. Since

Chapter Fourteen

the 1980s there have been those who have been concerned that preaching is going the way of the rotary phone, it is becoming obsolete. For the Apostle Paul, preaching held an indispensable place in salvation history:

> Everyone who calls on the name of the Lord shall be saved. How then can they call on the one they have not believed in? And how can they believe in the one of whom they have not heard? And how can they hear without a preacher? And how can anyone preach unless they are sent?

The key cog in that soteriological continuum is the preacher. According to Paul, there is no calling if there is no believing; there is no believing if there is no hearing; there is no hearing if there is no preaching; and there is no preaching if there is no sending. In the center of that enterprise is the preacher. That high regard for preaching, as it is conveyed in scripture, has been challenged in post-modern Christendom.

Can the world now hear without a preacher? Are they even hearing the preacher? Does preaching, as we have known it, have a place in the assembly of society? Does preaching still matter in the establishment of love and justice? In the establishment of love and justice, education seems to matter. Technology and social media have definitely carved out a niche. The popularity of the NFL and NBA shows that sports are a permanent fixture in our society. It is clear that celebrities and musical icons have a voice. About three years ago "Black Lives Matter" demonstrated that protests still had a voice. There is sufficient evidence that politics still matters. Does preaching have a place in society and in the church? Has it been knocked off of its lofty perch?

For the most part, preaching is held in high regard by those of us who do it. We love to hear great preaching and we rate who the best preachers are in the African American tradition. We attend certain conferences depending on who is preaching. But in the scheme of human living does it have a place? In Black churches preaching used to be the center of the church's life. But that may not be the case anymore. Has preaching been replaced by praise and worship? Has its centrality been eclipsed by creative programming? There was a time when great preaching equaled a large church. This is not the case anymore. There is no longer a correlation between effective preaching and size of church. In times past, if you knew of a large church, that also meant that there was a "prince" in the pulpit. A friend of mine recently told me that she joined a particular church in one of our large cities. I asked her, "Why that particular church." She said, "Well the preacher is solid, but the praise and worship experience is excellent." I don't place a value judgment on that, but that is where we are.

The preaching world both in the church and the academy has been hit by the acorn, and it appears as though the sky is falling. Some scholars say preaching has run its course. They say the craft served its purpose back when we were a word-based culture; but today a monologue seems like an outdated mode of communication. For some it's not even a matter of whether or not the Word (logos) matters; the question is do "words" matter? In an image-based culture, do words matter? As preachers we wrestle with the "what" of preaching; perhaps there needs to be some a priori wrestling with the "that" of preaching. They say the craft , but today a monologue seems like an outdated mode of communication. For some it's not even a matter of whether or not the Word (logos) matters; the question is do "words" matter? In an image-based culture, do words matter? As preachers we wrestle with the "what" of preaching; perhaps there needs to be some priori wrestling with the "that" of preaching. We spend time on what we should be preaching; perhaps we need to be asking if we should be preaching at all. Our concern is often with "res significata"- that is "things signified"; some others are more interested in "modus significundi"- that is "the way of signifying." While we spend our time on hermeneutics, exegesis, style and delivery, there may be a larger or piercing issue: relevance! We may be wondering about what we preach to help in the establishment of love and justice; the real issue right now is will and does preaching even make a difference.

The recent concern about the place and future of preaching is justified. The cultural climate in which preaching exists justifies the question. Some of the societal trends and traits demand that we take this issue seriously. In the book,

Chapter Fourteen

The Future of Preaching, edited by Geoffrey Stevenson, Roger Standing, in discussing the ethos and atmosphere of British culture, says that the current culture is characterized by entertainment, narrative, consumerism, distrust for authority, celebrity, and virtual relationship. Most of what he argues concerning British culture is true about American culture. When it comes to entertainment, British society seeks to amuse itself to death; the American scene is no different. Human beings have to constantly be amused by something. Have you noticed the proliferation of television screens? I was in a taxi in New York City, and there was a screen into the back seat, and I could watch TV. I go to the bathroom of some restaurants and there are flat screens on the walls; God forbid that I miss anything as I am in the bathroom. Our society needs to be constantly amused! This affects our preaching!

Connected to this is the emphasis on celebrity. People who entertain us, whether it be on the basketball court or on a movie screen, are held in higher regard than those who inform us. Our heroes used to be those who serve and sacrifice; today's heroes are those who make us feel good. The impact on preaching and the preacher is obvious.

Just like British culture, American society is also obsessed with "narrative." So-called reality shows about popular families reveal how much we want to know people's stories. Roger Standing argues that it would be unwise for preaching to ignore the all-pervasiveness of narrative and the overwhelming interest to know the "story."

Standing is correct by saying consumerism continues to identify Western civilization. In quoting an article in *The Chicago Tribune* in 1986, the author says that:

> We've become a nation measuring out our lives in shopping bags and nursing psychic ills through retail therapy…we make trips to the mall (or go online) to buy things we don't need with money we don't have to impress people we don't like."

This sense of consumerism affects preaching.

In addition to this, there is a fundamental distrust of the motives of those in authority that especially characterizes the mindset of millennials. "Trust has to be earned rather than just given as a mark of deference." This mindset has brought into the question the place and primacy of preaching and preacher.

Finally, Standing points out that virtual relationships are an obvious hallmark of contemporary culture. Virtual reality, which may not be reality at all, has replaced the actual hearer who sits in pews to hear the preacher. There are those who "stream" live services who really believe they are a part of the congregation. In one way or another, all of these realities contribute to the question as to whether or not preaching has a present place or a future role in the direction of human society.

The cultural climate which impacts the primacy and future of preaching is put differently by "Emerging Church" pastor, Dan Kimball. He uses the soil analogy in describing the differences between a person being raised in a modern vs. postmodern culture:

The so-called nutrients of modern soil include monotheism, rationality, religion, proposition, systematic, locality, individualism, and truth. These are the kinds of nutrients that were in the soil of my upbringing... Conversely, the postmodern soil is comprised of pluralism, the experiential, the mystical, narrative, fluidity, globalism, communalism/tribalism, and subjective preference. (*Preaching and the Emerging Church*, p.28)

The nutrients in the soil shape the world and the minds of the people who live in this world. And these nutrients impact how or even whether people "hear" preaching anymore.

The concern is justified because of the state of culture; it is also legitimate because of the nature of preaching itself. Preaching, as we have known it and practiced it, is a "word" phenomenon. At the heart of the "euangelion" and "kerygma" is speech. To preach is to "herald" good news. Preaching involves words, and as Fred Craddock points out, there has been a loss in the confidence of the power of words to convey reality. In television advertising, images and soundtracks have replaced words. Craddock, in his work *As One Without Authority*, says that there are six factors that have led to the loss in the confidence of the power of words: 1) people are bombarded by so many words; 2) the contempt for religious language in a scientific age; 3) the effect of television on the human sensorium, through which the aural has been replaced by the visual; 4) the crisis of the confidence in the power of the pulpit by those who occupy it; 5) Christian belief, which had been a part of Western consciousness since before the Middle Ages, is no longer reinforced by the society at large; and 6) talking to people about the most serious issues in life always has been difficult and remains so.

Because of the climate of the culture in which we preach and because of the nature of preaching itself, I understand the "chicken little-like" panic. Indeed, an acorn has fallen. However, I contend that the concern about the obsolescence of preaching may be premature. I am in agreement with Craddock who says in the opening lines of *As One Without Authority*, "We are all aware that in countless courts of opinion the verdict on preaching has been rendered and the sentence passed…" He quickly goes on to say, "All this slim volume asks is a stay of execution until one other witness is heard." I am asking for the same stay of execution that Craddock asks for. It may be foolish to think that preaching still has a place in the pantheon of societal significance, but preaching is foolishness anyway. But according to Paul, God chose to save the world through the foolishness. A part of the issue is that we expect preaching to receive mainstream acceptance. It is still a stumbling block to some and foolishness to others. The preaching of the gospel is yet foolishness!

Talk of the death and demise of preaching is premature. Preaching may be in the "ER", but it's still alive. However, the future fruitfulness and effectiveness of preaching (in the establishment of love and justice) may be dependent on five words or ideas: *authenticity, authority, variety, contextuality, and spirituality*. To a greater or lesser degree these ideas are embodied by the role that the prophet Jehaziel plays in 2 Chronicles Chapter 20. In this narrative, the prophet Jehaziel, in the midst of a national crisis, "stands in the assembly." King Jehoshaphat hears that a military alliance is on its way to attack Judah. Initially the King panics. From panic the King decides to pray. (Not a bad

Chapter Fourteen

move, from panic to prayer). He gathers the people together and they pray. After praying they wait to hear from God. After some period of waiting, the prophet stands in the assembly. That he stands, how he stands, and what he says gives birth to these six ideas which may aid in preserving the "shelf-life" of preaching. There's nothing new about any of these words or ideas, however, a reemphasis on them is vital for preaching in the twenty-first century.

First of all, there is this idea of **authenticity**. This particular emphasis rises above the confines of this biblical narrative. The twenty-first century preacher will need to convey a sense of real humanity. The listener in the pew and society no longer desire to hear a bishop, reverend, or doctor who is some superhuman who has feet of gold. They want to hear a brother or sister who have feet of clay. The listener wants to know: "Have you been where we've been preacher? Do you know our sorrows, hurts, confusions, joys, guilt, confusion, and doubt?" The sermon listener in this century doesn't simply want to know what seminary you've been to; they want to know, "Have you spent any days in Heartbreak Hotel?"

In the words of Martin Buber, preaching of today and tomorrow will need to establish an "I-thou" relationship, and not an "I-it" relationship. The "I-thou" relationship with the congregation forces the preacher to preach through his/her vulnerabilities. When the Lord needs a voice for the people who are stranded at the rivers of Babylon wondering, how they can sing the Lord's song in a strange land, the Lord does not import a preacher from out of town; the Lord raises up an Ezekiel who can identify with the people because he has been with them!

The "preachy" voice and the "preachy" persona that once worked for most of the twentieth century is not as effective now. To hear a C.L. Franklin or a Gardner Taylor mount the pulpit was to hear a majestic voice that emanated from above. The voice heard in this century is a voice that emanates from below, even though it has a word from above. A conversational tone of voice resonates with the hearer of our times.

There is a reason that God calls a preacher from amongst the people. God desires that the preacher be in relationship with people in order to be an authentic, transparent voice.

Obviously, our transparency does not go to the extreme. We don't "bleed" on the people. We don't use the preaching moment to simply vent our frustrations. The preaching moment is not our therapy session. We don't make ourselves the heroes of all of our personal illustrations. However, we are cracked clay pots; and the treasure of the gospel is contained in our brokenness. There is nothing wrong with that brokenness showing up in our preaching. The Lord deposits the treasure in clay, cracked pots, because the people listening are broken. The brokenness of the preacher resonates with the brokenness of the hearer. In 2 Chronicles 20, Jehaziel is with the people. He also knows of the fears of this oncoming military attack. There is no helicopter that drops him off in the assembly. He has gathered with them, and he comes from them as their voice.

On the other end of the spectrum, the idea of **authority** is critical going forward. The twenty-first century preacher needs to embrace a "humble authority." This might seem ironic in light of the anti-authority age in which we live, and in light of the distrust that millennials seem to have with figures of authority. The irony is that there is yet a need for the listener to know that the preacher comes with a certain boldness and is not sheepish about what is being said. The twenty-first century still demands a confident voice, even if it is more conversational in its approach.

Jehaziel stands in the assembly. He is confident about what his role is. The national crisis in which the people find themselves necessitates a voice of authority. The late Dr. A. Louis Patterson Jr. used to say to us as preachers, "You're the only one standing, so why don't you preach a little while." The preacher can stand in a confidence and authority that pushes him/her into the pulpit even when there is an inward reticence. There are days when the preacher wrestles with a worthiness to stand during the sacred moment; that is the time for the preacher to embrace the vocational authority that he/she has.

The authority in which the preacher stands is a humble authority. We don't "Lord" it over the people. Our pulpit authority is baptized in humility. It is humble because the preacher is conscious of his tainted, tinged, and tarnished humanity. Consciousness of personal, existential failure dismantles arrogance. The preacher stands in the shoes of Isaiah who came to the conclusion, "woe is me." The same Isaiah who is "wowed" by God's majesty, is "woed" by his own depravity. The authority is humble authority because it is derived authority. After calling the disciples, Jesus sits them down and gives them "authority". The word for "power or authority" in that passage is "exousia." It is not "dunamis." "Dunamis is an inherent ability that is native and natural. Exousia is a derived ability based on a connection with something larger than you are. Jehaziel stands because he has a connection with something bigger than he is! The preacher of the twenty-first century can stand because of a connection with something bigger!

The third word is **variety**. The prophet Jehaziel stands up and says what he has to say. Words, as direct address, are the medium through which Jehaziel conveys reality. Effective, fruitful preaching of the twenty-first century will need to be comfortable with a variety of approaches. The preacher cannot be enslaved to one particular style or approach. It is true that preachers need to be true to who they are and what they are comfortable with. However, I cannot make an idol out of my style and approach. There are times when I have to stretch who I am and come at the preaching moment with a different approach. The exhibition and exercise of your particular preaching style is less important than the communication of the kerygma.

My early preaching ministry was influenced by the likes of some effective expository preachers. I was drawn to the expository approach of an A. Louis Patterson and an E.K. Bailey. I appreciated the logical flow of exposition and the memorable alliteration. I came to believe that that was the only way to preach. However, I discovered that weaving in narrative and metaphorical preaching added necessary variety that enhanced the preaching moment. I started noticing that hearers resonated more with the stories than they did with propositions and points. Therefore, my deductive approach to preaching periodically gave way to a more inductive mode.

Going forward there are some approaches that some preachers are experimenting with and may be worth noting. For example, there is more experimentation with multi-sensory preaching. Multi-sensory preaching, as opposed to mono-sensory preaching, has proven to be effective in some circles. Mono-sensory preaching is preaching that is word only and it speaks to sense of hearing. Multisensory preaching, which has become particularly popular in the so-called Emerging Church movement, aims at stimulating the senses of sight and sound. A friend and colleague of mine preached a sermon series right after the Olympic games in Brazil, entitled, "Lessons from the Games." It was a four or five-week series in which he showed clips from the highlight moments of the Olympic games, and then he would proceed to connect those clips to biblical texts and preach them. That is a multi-sensory approach. It may not be something to depend on every week, because even that approach can become predictable, and I still believe the spoken word can stand on its own. But it is a way to periodically inject some freshness into the preaching moment. Jesus was multi-sensory in some of his preaching. After hearing the accusation concerning the woman who was caught in adultery coming from the religious leaders, Jesus writes on the ground and then he speaks. He appealed to both sight and sound. And subsequently the accusers walked away leaving their stones as markers of the graves where they buried their self-righteousness. The age in which we preach does call for a variety of approaches to the preaching moment.

The fourth idea is that of **contextuality**. In order to enhance the fruitfulness and effectiveness of twenty-first century preaching, the preacher must preach with a consciousness of the world around her/him. When Jehaziel stands up he tells the people not to be afraid of the vast army that is approaching, because the battle is not theirs, it's the Lord's. He at least shows that he is aware of what is happening around God's people.

I was recently on a flight during which we were experiencing significant turbulence. The voice of a flight attendant was coming through the intercom system as she was telling us about the snacks they had for purchase. She ran down the list of complimentary beverages available. Her voice was cheery and perky. There was no mention of the turbulence we were experiencing.

Chapter Fourteen

I'm looking around, wondering if she was aware of what was occurring around us. It was as though we were living inside this plane, inside this self-contained reality without any connection to the turbulence around us. Twentieth century preaching cannot resemble that. The word we preach has to take into account the world around it.

This is nothing new. Preaching has always borne the burden of needing to be contextual. But this is especially important now. Young adult listeners particularly, want to know that there is some connection between the truth of the gospel and the turbulence in society. The gospel is always preached in context. It never exists in a vacuum. John's inimitable prelude says that God set the precedent for contextuality. It reminds us that the "logos" always becomes "sarx" (flesh). The logos becomes sarx, and dwells amongst us. In the words of Eugene Peterson, "It moves into the neighborhood." Every time we stand the "word should become flesh." Our preaching should "move into the neighborhood in which it preaches." This is what Samuel Proctor used to call "the ecology of the sermon." The sermon exists in a certain climate and environment. I was closing out a revival in Atlanta, after the Tuesday that Donald Trump was elected president, and I was ready to ride one of my "horses." But there was no way that I could preach and divorce the sermon from the climate of the church, community, and the nation, so I had to do something else. In his classic work, *Certain Sound of the Trumpet*, Proctor says that:

> When the sermon begins with the issue that troubles us, the condition that haunts us, the ideas that annoy us, the statistics that embarrass us, the personality traits that destroy us, the moral vacuum that threatens us, the false idols that seduce us, the new questions in science or medicine or education that confuse us, the dullness of spirit that defeats us, the estrangement from God that causes us to hunger and thirst for the bread of life and the living water, we are right there where everyone else is.

Chapter Fourteen

All of this notwithstanding, in our attempt to be contextual, the preacher does not simply reflect the world around him or her; the preacher offers an alternative world. Our style and content occurs within a certain context, but it does more than reflect that context; it rises above it. Walter Brueggemann says that all week people have been living in a "prose-flattened world. Our preaching should offer a daring, imaginative alternative." When the prophet Jehaziel begins to speak he says, "This is what the Lord says…" All week the people have heard what everyone else has said. When they come to the house of God, they need to hear someone say, "This is what the Lord says." All week the people have heard what everyone else has said. When they come to the house of God, they need to hear someone say, "This is what the Lord says." They've heard what the doctor has said, but "This is what the Lord says." They've heard what the boss has said, but "This is what the Lord says." The people come to hear "news from another network."

Finally, and most importantly, twenty-first century preaching has to be influenced by the "world of the Spirit." This is the idea of spirituality.

As in ages past, twenty-first century preaching is born of human work and born of Spirit-influence. Cleophus LaRue has an insightful chapter included in his book *I Believe I'll Testify*, entitled, "The Shape of Colored Preaching in the Twenty-first Century" in which he notes that:

> We have always known that there is more to the preaching life than the realities of the empirical world that we can see and touch. We have always known that there is more to preaching than interpretive strategies and correct biblical exegesis. In dealing with mystery there are other dimensions that simply cannot be accounted for even when you have followed every step of the exegesis process... still there is the asking after God that must come before the sermon is complete.

Preaching is both "learned and given."

The irony of all of this is that the pressure is not on us to keep preaching alive. Yes, it is incumbent upon us to do our work. Yes, it is incumbent upon us to do our exegetical work. But, when it comes down to it, it is the Spirit of God who breathes life into our feeble, fractured words. No matter how much work you do, the sermon is flat unless the Spirit breathes on it. Jehaziel had nothing meaningful to say until the Spirit came upon him. His resume is read. We learn who is daddy and granddaddy are. We learn that he was a Levite. But nothing really happens until "the Spirit of the Lord came upon him." When the Spirit of the Lord came upon him, he was able to preach until Jehoshaphat and the people mustered up enough courage to march out of the valley of timidity onto the mountaintop of courage. When the Spirit of the Lord came upon him, he was able to preach until the people who had been panicking began to praise. And when they started praising in one place, God started setting ambushes in another place. Preaching has as future! The sky is not falling!

Biography

Dr. Jerry M. Carter serves as the 14th Pastor of the Calvary Baptist Church of Morristown, New Jersey. During his tenure, the impact of his ministry has extended well beyond Calvary and the Morristown community. He is a dedicated theologian and a highly sought after lecturer, keynote speaker, and revivalist, who has been invited to share the Gospel on various platforms throughout the country.

Dr. Carter received his BA from Denison University, his MDiv. from Princeton Theological Seminary, and his Ph.D. from Drew Theological School, and he is the recipient of the Expository Preaching Award from Princeton.

Those who "sit" under Pastor Carter's preaching, teaching, and tutelage benefit greatly from his anointed divining and proclamation of the Word of God and its profound ability to change lives. With a prescience of eventual ramifications, Dr. Carter founded the *How Shall They Hear* Preaching Conference to further encourage, prepare and strengthen those with "beautiful feet" who would bring "Good News" to the world.

Dr. Carter's adjunct assignments include Princeton Seminary, The Drew Theological School, and New Brunswick Seminary all in New Jersey and The Dewitt Proctor School of Theology in Richmond, VA. He is the author of two books: *The Empowered Life: Living Well in the Spirit*, and *The Journey to Purpose: Navigating Your Spiritual Path*, in addition to being a contributor to *The New Interpreter's Handbook of Preaching, Oxford Sermons Volume III Evangelizing the Black Male in the 21st Century and the African American Pulpit*.

Dr. Carter currently serves as the President of the African American Clergy Association of Morris County, New Jersey, and he is the proud father of three children: Jerry M. III, Zachary Daniel, and Camille Ashley.

Bibliography

Barth, Karl. *Homiletics*. Louisville, Westminster/John Knox. 1991

Bonhoeffer, Dietrich. *Worldly Preaching: Lectures on Homiletics*. New York, Crossroads. 1991

Brueggemann, Walter. *Finally Comes the Poet: Daring Speech for Proclamation*. Minneapolis, Fortress Press. 1989

Brueggemann, Walter. *The Word Militant: Preaching a Decentering Word*. Minneapolis, Fortress Press. 2007

Buttrick, George A. *The Parables of Jesus*. Grand Rapids, Michigan, Baker Book House. 1973

Davis, H. Grady. *Design for Preaching*. Minneapolis, Minnesota, Fortress Press. 1958

Frazier, E. Franklin. *The Negro Church in America*. New York, Schocken Books. 1974

Jeremias, Joachim. *The Parables of Jesus: Second Revised Edition*. New York. SCM Press, Ltd. 1954

Larue, Cleophus J. *The Heart of Black Preaching*. Louisville, Westminster/John Knox. 2000

Levingston, Steven. *Kennedy and King: The President, The Pastor, and the Battle Over Civil Rights*. New York/ Boston, Hachette Books. 2017

Lischer, Richard. *Theories of Preaching: Selected Readings in the Homiletical Tradition*. North Carolina. The Labyrinth Press. 1987

Massey, James Earl. *The Sermon in Perspective: A Study of Communication and Charisma*. Michigan. Baker Book House. 1976

Proctor, Samuel D. *The Certain Sound of the Trumpet: Crafting a Sermon of Authority*. Valley Forge, Pennsylvania, Judson Press. 1994

Proctor, Samuel D. *We Have This Ministry: The Heart of The Pastor's Vocation*. Valley Forge, Pennsylvania, Judson Press. 1996

Raboteau, Albert J. *A Fire in The Bones: Reflections on African-American Religious History*. Boston, Beacon Press. 1995

Root, Andrew. *The Pastor in a Secular Age*. Michigan, Baker Academic. 2019

Spurgeon, C.H. *Lectures to My Students: The 28 Lectures, Complete and Unabridged*. Michigan, Zondervan Publishing House. 1954

Stevenson, Geoffrey. *The Future of Preaching*. London UK, SCM Press. 2010

Taylor, Barbara Brown. *The Preaching Life*. Boston, Cowley Publications. 1993

Taylor, Gardner C. *The Words of Gardner Taylor: Volume 1*. Valley Forge, Pennsylvania, Judson Press. 1999

Webb, Stephen H. *The Divine Voice: Christian Proclamation and The Theology of Sound.* Grand Rapids, Michigan, Brazos Press. 2004

Wilkerson, Isabel. *Caste: The Origins of Our Discontents.* New York, Random House. 2020

Wilmore, Gayraud S. *Black Religion and Black Radicalism: An Interpretation of the Religious History of Afro-American People.* New York, Orbis Books. 1973

Wilson, Jared C. "The 5C's of Preaching". www.thegospelcoalition.org